celebrate the
SEASON®
2016

contents

fall

6 Honor nature's autumnal gifts with projects that welcome in colors and symbols of the season. Pumpkins, leaves, pinecones, and more inspire home decor while unique decorations make the most of Thanksgiving and other fall gatherings. During this season of thanks, friends and family will be grateful for your talents.

trims

34 Create a magical wonderland that invites everyone who gathers in your home to feel the spirit of the season. You're sure to earn awards for best-dressed table, most festive tree, and unsurpassed holiday decorations using dozens of artful ideas in this chapter. Use your hues, put your spin on it—make this Christmas memorable!

food

90 Serve some of the season's favorite dishes to make holiday meals extra special. Planning menus is creative with *Better Homes and Gardens* Kitchen-Tested Recipes on hand. Appetizers, main dishes, desserts galore—so many options to try! Guests will rave about your cooking—so get ready to receive their compliments.

gifts

118 Bring on cheer with handmade gifts that ring with thoughtfulness. From tasty tidbits packaged in ever-so-clever wraps to personalized crafted projects, these gifts will be welcomed and adored. You might leap at trying at new techniques, such as woodburning, coiling, or hypotrochoid drawing.

kids

138 Inspire young creativity and participation. Show kids how to craft with colorful papers, pens, paints, and all shapes and sizes of pasta. Then when it comes to accepting credit for wondrous tree decorations, package add-ons and wraps, holiday cards, and table trims, youngsters will glow.

in a twinkling

Easy on time and fun to create, these projects encourage making several to share.

Meredith Consumer Marketing
Consumer Marketing Product Director: Heather Sorensen
Consumer Marketing Product Manager: Wendy Merical
Consumer Marketing Billing/Renewal Manager: Tami Beachem
Business Director: Ron Clingman
Senior Production Manager: Al Rodruck

Waterbury Publications, Inc.
Editorial Director: Lisa Kingsley
Creative Director: Ken Carlson
Associate Editors: Tricia Bergman, Mary Williams
Associate Design Director: Doug Samuelson
Production Assistant: Mindy Samuelson
Contributing Editor: Sue Banker
Contributing Copy Editor: Terri Fredrickson
Contributing Proofreader: Peg Smith

Better Homes and Gardens® Magazine
Editor in Chief: Stephen Orr
Executive Editor: Oma Blaise Ford
Managing Editor: Gregory H. Kayko
Creative Director: Jennifer D. Madara
Senior Deputy Editor, Food and Entertaining: Nancy Wall Hopkins

Meredith National Media Group
President: Tom Harty

Meredith Corporation
Chairman and Chief Executive Officer: Stephen M. Lacy

In Memoriam: E.T. Meredith III (1933–2003)

Editor's Letter

I'll never forget the year we spent Christmas away from home. There we were with two young children in the sands of Florida rather than in Iowa snow. I worried and wondered: Would it feel like the holiday?

To ensure it would, I pared down stuffing personal items in my suitcase just enough to fit in a small silver tree, lightweight plastic ornaments, a few strings of lights, and dozens of paper snowflakes cut from bright printed papers for the walls and windows of our hotel room.

On Christmas Eve, once the kids were sound asleep from a busy day at the theme park, this elf transformed our cookie-cutter hotel room into a joyful wonderland.

When the kids awoke, there was no question that Santa had found them, even miles from home. Although the decorations were simple and hand-crafted, they made that Christmas morning very special.

That's where *Better Homes and Gardens® Celebrate the Season®* comes in. It offers hundreds of ways—big and small—to make holidays amazingly meaningful. From wondrous decorations calling on a variety of techniques to delicious kitchen-tested recipes to handcrafted gifts to super-fun projects for kids, *Celebrate the Season* provides the magic to pull off memorable holiday gatherings.

So wherever your holiday season finds you—at home or on the road—bring on merriment inspired by these festive ideas. Sharing personal and thoughtful touches makes the season as magical as a theme park.

Wishing you an extraordinary holiday season,

Lue Barker

A CHANGING PALETTE

fall

Enjoy The Bounty
Autumn offers a refreshing switch
in colors and seasonal motifs that
sparks creativity indoors and out.

Late Additions

Gourds and pumpkins—even cabbage and cauliflower heads—transform summer-weary planters into autumnal delights.

Feast for the Eyes

Branch out from the usual cast of characters when gathering ingredients to dress up a window box for fall. In addition to gnarly gourds and pumpkins, employ sculptural veggies, including chartreuse Romanesco broccoli, squat Cipollini onions, basketball-size cabbage heads, and strings of Brussels sprouts on stalks. If weather is cool, vegetables can last two to three weeks—plenty of time for a party and then some.

Skirt the Subject

It's easy to give a potted mum deserved oomph. Just transplant it or set it in a slightly larger container then surround it with small pumpkins and gourds in compatible hues. The "miniskirt" also hides stems at the base. Shop for tightly budded plants for the longest bloom.

Fall

In Good Company

In fall, pots with frost-tolerant plants such as kale, sedge, and mums, stay fresh well into cold weather. Dyed dried oats add spiky flair.

Fall Revival

A rosemary plant held over from summer gets a late-season refresh with a fringe of mums and striped and nubby gourds that seem to tumble out of the pot. Unify various sizes and shapes of gourds with a muted color palette of pale green, gray, and white.

Turkey Time Triumph

Celebrate Thanksgiving with a blend of natural, lovingly crafted accents that show guests how much they are appreciated.

A Pop of Plaid

A soft plaid scarf makes the perfect runway for this natural display. Choose one with contrasting color, such as turquoise, to set off orange, gold, and brown.

After-Dinner Delights

Votive candleholders do double-duty holding candy. Choose candies wrapped in seasonal tones to blend with the color palette. Tuck in a freshly washed leaf for the finishing touch.

All Set
Create a feast for the eyes with help from Mother Nature. Arrange small pumpkins and autumn flowers for a dramatic centerpiece.

Sweet Stacks
Foil-wrapped cookies, homemade or purchased, are welcomed favors. Stack a few then tie with ribbon for an extra-special touch. If the stacks tend to slip, secure with tiny pieces of double-sided tape before tying with ribbon.

Spell It Out
Display a message of thanks by stringing galvanized metal letters onto ribbon. If letters have hangers on the back, thread ribbon through them. Or, if necessary, drill holes near the top for stringing. In lieu of a bow, knot extra ribbons to the ends.

Corn Canister Favors
Bid farewell to guests with a much-appreciated canister of popping corn. A blend of colorful kernels is enticing.

Autumnal Flair

A twig wreath is the background for tucking dried and fresh seasonal bounty. Indian corn, gourds, and fresh-picked leaves provide a flurry of color and texture. For a longer-lasting version, use artificial leaves. If desired, hot-glue pinecones and acorns to the arrangement.

Initially Yours

This Thanksgiving, use chalkboard tags and letter stickers to direct each guest to his or her seat at the table. Use a stencil brush and metallic paint to stipple the edges of each tag. Thread each tag with ribbon and drape a tag onto plates or use them as napkin rings.

Candy-Go-'Round

Set a tart pan on each dinner plate and fill with seasonal candies to encircle a small gourd. Enjoy the candies after dinner or offer clear plastic favor bags to slide in the goodies for guests to enjoy later.

Cheery Cheers

Single-serve wine bottles tied with seasonal ribbon bows add a festive touch to the Thanksgiving table.

Pinecone Pretties

Earthy and full of texture, these intriguing Mother Nature finds fit in perfectly with autumn decor.

Sticks and Cones

Textural pinecones and sliced branches pair for artful seasonal decoration. Hot-glue items onto a grapevine wreath and finish with a burlap bow topped with a large round pinecone.

Touched by Nature

A single pinecone makes a stunning embellishment on an unadorned napkin ring. First adhere ribbon to a plain napkin ring, allowing edges of the ring to show. Hot-glue a squat pinecone on ribbon ends to cover the seam.

Autumn Charger

Inexpensive plastic gold chargers get a boost to designer status with a few quick, crafty touches. First, coat the top of the charger with decoupage medium. Press on a piece of burlap cut slightly larger than the charger. Smooth any wrinkles and trim off excess; let dry. Hot-glue cording trim around the edge. Arrange pinecones, wheat, and artificial greenery into a small spray; glue into place. Add a ribbon bow to complete. Keep placement near the edge so a plate will fit easily in the center.

Pretty Placecard

Bring elegance to the table with ornate placecards. Fold 5×3½-inch patterned paper in half. Write a guest's name on a 1½×½-inch piece of white paper and glue it onto placecard slightly below center and to the right. Trim with a snippet of ribbon and five mini pinecones in star formation, then dot in the center with a putka pod.

Turning Over a New Leaf

Crunchy, colorful leaves and showy branches are delightful joys of autumn. These easy projects bring them indoors.

Falling for Clay

Create little leaf dishes to display small items and bring a hint of fall into your decor. To make them, roll out air-dry clay on a piece of linen (for texture) to about ⅛-inch thickness. Use leaf-shape cookie cutters to cut out clay, then place leaves, linen pattern up, on parchment. Let dry about two days. When completely dry, paint leaves with a mixture of two parts liquid fabric dye to one part water, allowing some natural clay color to show through if desired.

Autumn Glow

These lanterns are so much greater than the sum of their parts. Cut waxed paper into four 5×12-inch pieces, then fold in half to 5×6 inches. Place leaves—fresh, dried, faux, or even cut-out printed images—inside the folded waxed paper then press with an iron on low heat to seal. Tape the four sides together with decorative tape to form a lantern, then place a battery-operated votive inside. *Note:* Waxed paper can burn. Use only battery-operated candles.

Make an Entrance

Add glam to the front door with an easy-to-make leaf swag. Use a foam brush to cover leaves one at a time with crafts glue, then coat with glitter, and shake off excess. Cut wire-edge ribbon into 20-inch pieces and hot-glue a glittered leaf to the end of each. Gather ribbon ends, knot the top, and trim the ends.

Bowls of Plenty

Faux leaves shape up beautifully into light-as-a-feather bowls. To make one, blow up a balloon (the bigger the balloon, the bigger the bowl) and rest it in a bowl. Cover the top of the balloon and the right sides of the leaves with decoupage medium. Layer the leaves face-down on the balloon to form a bowl shape. Brush more decoupage medium on the backs of the leaves. Let dry overnight. Once dry, poke a hole in the balloon to release the air, then discard the balloon.

Add a Little Spice

Usher in changing colors and cooler temps with a bounty of handmade touches for your home.

It's a Wrap

A miniature pumpkin gets texture from yarn and burlap.

WHAT YOU'LL NEED
Serrated knife
3-inch-diameter foam ball
Crafts knife
Scissors
¾×1 inch cork bottle stopper
Chunky orange yarn
White paper
Hot-glue gun and glue sticks
Textured cardstock: moss green
Burlap
Fine-tip marking pen: black

WHAT YOU DO
1. Use a serrated knife to cut a thin slice off the edge of the foam ball. The flat edge will be the bottom of the pumpkin.
2. Use a crafts knife or the closed pointed end of scissors to hollow out a hole in the top of the ball to fit the narrow end of a cork bottle stopper. Hot-glue a cork bottle stopper into the hole for the stem.
3. Glue the yarn end at the base of the cork. Horizontally wrap the yarn around the cork in a spiral, gluing as you wrap. Continue to glue and wrap yarn to cover the ball.
4. Trace leaf pattern on page 152 onto white paper; cut out. Cut leaf from textured cardstock. Write a name or message on the leaf using a fine-tip marking pen. Glue cardstock leaf to burlap; trim, leaving a ⅛-inch burlap border around leaf. Glue leaf to the top of the pumpkin.

Round It Out

Announce the arrival of autumn at your door. Outfit the wreath with a miniature felt and burlap pennant banner, a cluster of felt roses, and artificial branches.

WHAT YOU'LL NEED
2½-inch-wide burlap ribbon
16-inch-diameter foam wreath form
Hot-glue gun and glue sticks
Burlap
White paper
Felt in moss green, brown, gold, and oatmeal
Large-eye tapestry needle
Oatmeal yarn
Artificial berry branches
Twine
1½-inch-wide satin ribbon: tan

WHAT YOU DO
COVER THE WREATH
1. Secure one end of burlap ribbon to the back of the foam wreath form with hot glue. Wrap ribbon around the wreath form, overlapping wraps to cover the form. Trim burlap ribbon end and glue to back of wreath.

MAKE THE ROSES AND LEAVES
1. Trace patterns on page 152 onto white paper; cut out. Cut two large leaves from moss green felt. Cut two large leaves from brown felt. Cut one small leaf from moss green felt. Cut one small leaf from brown felt.
2. Use a running stitch and oatmeal yarn to stitch an outline approximately ¼ inch from the edge of each felt leaf. Hot-glue each leaf to burlap, spacing shapes at least ½ inch apart; let dry. Cut around each leaf, leaving a ¼ inch burlap border around each leaf.
3. Cut sixteen 2-inch-diameter circles from gold felt. Referring to diagrams A, B, and C, make 16 roses. Vary tightness of rolls to make big or small roses.

MAKE THE PENNANT
1. Cut four triangles from oatmeal felt. Glue each triangle to burlap, spacing shapes at least ½ inch apart; let dry. Cut around each triangle, leaving a ¼-inch burlap border around each shape.

2. Cut four 12-inch lengths of twine. Shape and glue each piece of twine into a letter on each felt pennant triangle to spell "fall"; trim the ends.
3. Cut a 36-inch length of twine for pennant hanger. Glue the top edge of each pennant to the hanger.

EMBELLISH THE WREATH
1. Glue felt roses to the lower edge of the wreath in a tightly packed cluster. Glue one small and two large leaves along each side of the rose cluster.

2. Extend the banner across the center of the wreath and wrap twine ends around the wreath to the back. Adjust as needed; trim excess twine ends. Hot-glue ends to the back of wreath.
3. Trim each berry branch to desired length, then poke ends into burlap-covered wreath form along each side of the rose cluster. Bend branches as desired.
4. Tie a satin ribbon bow at the top for hanging.

Spell Bound

Welcome the season—and guests—with yarn-wrapped chipboard letters falling in just the right order. Mount each letter on burlap backing that fits a frame just large enough to hold each letter, then top with felt flowers, acorns, and leaves. The roses are made just like those on page 29.

WHAT YOU'LL NEED

8¾-inch-tall papier-mâché letters: fall
Yarn: moss green, oatmeal, brown, orange
Hot-glue gun and glue sticks
White paper
Felt: gold, moss green, brown
Tapestry needle
Burlap; hemp twine
4 wooden orange frames with 7½×9½-inch openings

WHAT YOU DO

1. Wrap each papier-mâché letter with a color of yarn, using a hot-glue gun to periodically secure yarn as you wrap.

Cover sides and ends of each letter by working outward from the center in a spiral.

2. Trace patterns on page 152 onto white paper; cut out. Cut three leaves from moss green felt. Cut one leaf and one acorn nut from gold felt. Cut two leaves and one acorn cap from brown felt.

3. Use a running stitch and oatmeal yarn to stitch an outline approximately ¼ inch from the edge of each felt leaf, acorn cap, and acorn nut. Hot-glue each leaf to burlap, spacing shapes at least ½ inch apart; let dry. Cut around each leaf, leaving a ¼-inch burlap border around each shape.

4. Hot-glue the acorn cap to the acorn nut, overlapping pieces slightly.

5. Draw four 2-inch-diameter circles onto gold felt, leaving ½ inch between circles. Referring to diagrams on page 29, make four roses. Vary tightness of the rolls to make big or small roses.

6. Hot-glue one rose and two leaves to the letter F. Hot-glue the acorn to the opening in the center of the letter A. Hot-glue one leaf and three roses to one L. Wrap hemp twine three times around the remaining letter L and tie the ends into a bow. Glue remaining three leaves below bow.

7. Remove backing from each frame and securely cover with burlap. Insert backing into frame. Hot-glue a letter onto the burlap backing of each frame.

Cork Creations

Squares-on-Squares Coasters

Brads in autumn hues dress up cork squares in minutes. Use an awl to gently poke a hole through the cork, centered and ½ inch in from the edge. Insert a square brad through the hole and bend out the prongs on the back. Repeat with four more brads, spacing equally along one edge. Cut felt slightly smaller than the cork and glue to the underside to prevent scratches.

Initial Drink Tags

Silent and lightweight, these glass charms add to gathering fun at gatherings. Purchase or cut out 1½-inch circles from cork. Punch a hole ¼ inch in from the edge and secure an eyelet. Use permanent marking pen to write an initial of each guest or let guests doodle their own. Use jute ties to carry out the natural theme.

Studded Table Mat

Used here for a candle mat, this technique also works well for place mats, tray inserts, and vase coasters. After cutting a cork circle to desired size, center and trace a circle onto the back, approximately ½ inch smaller in diameter. Use an awl to gently poke a hole through the cork on the drawn line. Insert a small round silver, brass, or copper brad through the hole then bend out the prongs on the back. Repeat around the entire circle, creating a color pattern, if desired, and spacing brads about ½ inch apart. Hot-glue cording around the edge and a felt circle on the underside.

Last-Minute Place Cards

Add a special touch to the party table with super-simple place cards. To make one, fold a 3½×3-inch piece of patterned paper in half, long ends together. Cut a 1×3-inch piece of cork and adhere to one side using two-sided tape. Use a permanent marking pen to write a name on the place card.

Wise Word Plaque

Make this meaningful message board in fewer than 10 minutes using a 10-inch length of 2×4 lumber. Cut off-white burlap the size of the board, pull threads on each side to make a ¼-inch fringe. Coat one side of the board with decoupage medium. Carefully center burlap on the board and smooth into place. Hot-glue 1½-inch letters to the board to spell "Be thankful." Using five pulled threads, align ends and tie into a bow. Make a second bow. Hot-glue bows in the space as shown. Trim top and bottom with narrow ribbon, hot-gluing ends on the back.

THERE'S MAGIC ALL AROUND

trims

Make It Merry
Big displays, little accents—however you trim for Christmastime, make memorable handcrafted decorations that spread the joy of the season.

Making the Rounds

Rough or refined—these embellishments turn ready-made wreaths into delightful decorations.

Magical Montage

A bewitching blend of twiggy, downy, and glossy elements makes this wreath singularly chic. Use the ready-made twig wreath as a canvas, and fresh foliage and dried floral stems as artistic media. Weave, wire, and glue cotton pods and holly and berry sprigs to fill the wreath surface with holiday hues. Like more glitz in the mix? Use a brush and metallic crafts paint to add sparkling highlights to stems, leaves, and pods.

Noel Notions

Look to your pantry and grocery store for seasonal staples to create stellar shapes. A moss-covered wreath provides a lushly cushioned backdrop for a series of stars formed with glued-in-place almonds and cranberries. Choose a wreath form with built-in embellishments—like this wreath's vine details—as a starting point, then finish with an assortment of highly textured, vibrantly colorful, and unexpected add-ons.

Bountiful Beauty

Broken twigs gathered from the yard adorn a grapevine wreath. White spray paint unites the twigs and gives the wreath a snow-dusted outlook. Tiny pinecones, a jute-ribbon bow, and fresh greenery underscore the wreath's woodland premise.

Avian Artistry

A reindeer moss wreath sets the stage for forest references, including sticks plucked from the yard and fabulously feathered birds. When adding embellishments, visually divide the wreath into quadrants to place and space the trimmings. Finish with a woven ribbon and a bow.

Trims

Gathered Together

Make a distinctive wreath for your front door by wiring together mini wreaths. These tiny cedars, grouped in a traditional tree shape, bid a merry welcome. Add a trunk and a ribbon bow as a tree topper and this clever arrangement is ready to hang. Like more color? Use wire to randomly attach mini plastic ornaments to the door decoration or hang one in the center of each mini wreath.

Shining Silhouette

Create a grand first impression by decking your entry with an evergreen wreath that shimmers when touched by sunbeams and starlight. This pleasingly plump front door decoration, features a balsam wreath accented by additional greenery then painted metallic silver. Frosty stems set the wreath aglow while fluffing out its already-generous form. Iridescent red beads glued amid the foliage and a silvery bow further enhance the wintry greeting.

Chalk Talk

Let the popular look of chalk paint flow onto jolly trims that share greetings for the season.

Merry Messages

Perk up a plastic ornament with a coat of black spray paint and doodles from a white paint pen for the look of chalk using a permanent smudge-free technique. After the spray paint is dry, write a word or phrase in the center of the ornament. If desired, print out the word(s) and use white transfer paper to place it on the ornament. Use a white paint pen to draw the letters. Using the photo as inspiration, frame the word or phrase with doodles.

Name Trees

Tiny tabletop trees decorate and guide guests to their seats. To make one, fold an 8½×11-inch piece of black cardstock in half lengthwise. Cut a triangular tree, leaving ½ inch uncut at the fold. Punch out a 1-inch circle from cardstock. Write the guest's name along the bottom of the tree and draw some ornaments. Draw a star on the circle and dot the edge. Use a glue stick to adhere the star to the top of the tree.

Festive Box Tops

Save the gift wrap and tape. These small boxes (available in crafts and party stores) are ready for gift exchanges with minimal decorating. Spray-paint the box or lid black; let dry. Use a white pen to customize with words, doodles, or designs. Add ribbon trim if desired.

Jolly Treat Jar

Transform a glass jar into a gift container with little effort. Cut a label shape from paper to fit one side of a jar. Center the design on the inside of the jar and tape in place. Using a paintbrush and black glass paint, brush on a coat of paint, using the cutout as a guide. Dip the eraser end of a pencil into the paint and dot around the painted design; let dry. Use a white paint pen to write on the label and dot each black dot; let dry.

Charming Charger

This charger, with myriad design options is used under a dinner plate or to take cookies to neighbors. To make one, spray-paint a charger with black paint and let dry. Using a white paint pen, draw dotted lines around the rim as shown. Write a holiday message between the dotted lines, using the photo for ideas. To use with large plates, write close to the edge to remain visible.

Ring Around the Napkin

Keep the chalk look going with these super easy napkin rings, which are made from sturdy wrapping paper tubes. Paint each black and let dry. Use a white paint marker to write a holiday message on each ring, with sayings all the same or unique. Use a hot-glue gun to attach a metallic silver chenille stem around each edge and a small ribbon bow at the top.

First Impressions

Share the season's magic with impressed clay trims that resemble etched stones.

Star Performance

Like snowflakes, each of these stars is unique. To achieve the soft look, choose oven-bake clay in subtle tones, such as light blue and muted denim. On a flat work surface covered with waxed paper, roll the clay to approximately ³⁄₁₆-inch thickness. Press snowflake and message stamps into the clay. Use cookie cutters to cut star shapes from the stamped clay. Make a small hanging hole at the top with a toothpick. Lift the stars with a spatula and place them on a baking sheet. Bake stars in the oven according to clay manufacturer's directions. When cooled, dip a wad of paper towel into a small amount of white paint and wipe across the surface to accent crevices; let the paint dry.

Terrific Topper

So pretty, these tags are gifts themselves! On a flat work surface covered with waxed paper, roll clay to approximately ³⁄₁₆-inches thickness. Press message stamps into the clay. Cut around each message in a tag shape using a sharp knife. Use a toothpick to make a small hole in one end. Place cutouts on a baking sheet and bake according to clay manufacturer's instructions; let cool. Dip a wad of paper towel into a small amount of white paint and wipe across the surface to accent crevices; let dry. Thread narrow ribbon through the hole and tie the topper onto a ribbon bow.

All Aglow

Dress up a plain candleholder with a pressed clay adornment, in the same manner as for the gift tag and ornaments. For the zigzag edge, carefully trim around the stamped word using decorative-edge scissors, then bake following manufacturer's directions. Use clear glue to attach the clay trim to the candleholder.

Signs of the Time

Call on favorite wintry images and adages for seasonal wall and tabletop art.

Pattern Play Poinsettias

A limited color palette and loads of pattern make this graphic artwork lively. Place a large plastic stencil over a 12×16-inch white canvas. Randomly sponge silver paint through the openings in stencil to create a worn-look pattern faint in some places, stronger in others; let dry. Using the patterns on page 156—and your own, if desired—cut petal shapes from red print papers. Cut leaf shapes from green and white polka-dot papers. For flower centers, cut circles around polka dots.

Trims

Lovely Lyrics

Turn the words of a favorite Christmas carol into seasonal art. Use a marking pen to write lyrics on approximately 1-inch strips of white cardstock; shade edges with brown chalk and set aside. Enlarge and trace the star pattern on page 156; cut out. Use the pattern to cut a star from patterned red scrapbook paper; chalk the edges. Use glue stick to adhere the star to a 12-inch-square black canvas. Use a white paint pen to dot around the edges of the star and to draw a freehand border on the perimeter.

Heavenly Harmony

A 12-inch-square shadowbox stylishly frames this sweet cherub. Use sheet music (or print one from the Internet) for the background; pin in place. Print two more sheets of music, reducing them to approximately 2 inches wide. Back with black paper and trim narrow borders. To make the angel, trace the patterns on page 155; cut out. Use the patterns to cut face, hands, and feet from peach paper; cut dress and sleeves from green papers. Cut a 6-inch circle from light green print paper for angel wings; fold to cut a snowflake. Cut snowflake, unfold, and cut in half. Referring to the photo for placement; position pieces on 8¼×7¾-inch white paper; adhere with glue stick. Use hot glue to attach artificial holly for a halo. Trim the design with adhesive gems.

Color Blast

Break away from traditional Christmas hues with melted acrylic bead decorations for vibrant to holiday decor.

Dancing Snowflakes

Decorative metal jar inserts give the appearance of wintry snowflakes. Fill the voids with color and the cutouts really stand out. To make a snowflake ornament, place a jar insert on a baking dish, right side down, as shown in Photo A. Cover the back with one color of transparent pony or tri beads as shown in Photo B. Preheat oven to 400°F and make sure the room is well ventilated. Carefully set the baking pan in the oven, making sure no beads roll off the lid insert. Bake until beads melt flat as shown in Photo C; let cool. Turn over the lid to reveal the design as shown in Photo D. Hot-glue a cord hanger to the back of the ornament. Hang snowflakes in a window, on a tree, or tie them to a package.

Notes for working on projects that involve the melting of plastic beads:

- Keep windows open for maximum ventilation during and after baking.
- To ensure the beads don't heat too long, check the oven often as different brands and sizes of beads melt at various rates. The beads also take longer to melt when used in a thick layer.
- To achieve a stained-glass look, purchase transparent beads, such as the pony and tri beads below. These beads are also available in opaque versions if solid colors are desired.
- To easily arrange beads, use a toothpick or skewer to assist in placement.

Trims

Kaleidoscope Place Mat

Brighten a winter white dinner table with dynamic place mats, formed completely of translucent pony beads. To make one, use a flat, round pizza pan with sides. Fill it completely with translucent pony beads in a variety of colors. With windows open and kitchen well-ventilated, preheat oven to 400°F. Place filled pizza pan in the oven and heat until beads are melted into a flat sheet. Remove from oven, let cool, and remove from pan.

Intriguing Insert

Give a canning jar an interesting twist by replacing the lid insert with a colorful plastic disk. Place the open lid on a baking dish, top down. Fill with pony or tri beads and bake in a 400° F oven until melted. Let cool. If disk pops out from lid, adhere with a few tiny drops of clear quick-dry glue.

Color-Drenched Candleholder

Let light shine through an abundance of color on a square glass candleholder. Add colorful "walls" by arranging translucent pony beads on a baking sheet in squares large enough to cover the sides of the candleholder. Melt in a 400° F oven until beads adhere together yet still have a rounded shape. Remove from oven and let cool. Use clear quick-dry glue to adhere a panel to each side of candleholder.

Trims

Ornamental Greetings

These clever cards are truly one of a kind. To make half-spheres, use a metal paint palette, available in crafts and art stores, as the mold. This method creates dimensional "ornaments" and allows you to prepare multiples at the same time. Fill each cup with translucent tri or pony beads as shown in Photo A. Melt in a 400°F oven until cups are filled. If necessary add a few more beads so shapes have flat bottoms once melted, as shown in Photo B. Let cool; pop shapes out of pan as shown in Photo C. Hot-glue a plastic half-sphere to cardstock. Back to silver perforated paper and then to a card. Shape a silver chenille stem to outline ornament; cut to size, then hot-glue in place. Make a cord loop for hanger; hot-glue ends to top of ornament. Tie a cord bow and glue in place.

Sparkling Wreath

Create a holiday wreath that glistens in sunlight. To easily make a ring shape, use an angel food pan for the mold. Press aluminum foil into the bottom to prevent beads from leaking through seams in the pan. Fill the bottom with clear and translucent green tri beads. Place in a 400°F oven until beads begin to melt together but still have texture; remove from oven. Add translucent red pony beads to the design to look like berries, placing individually or in groups of three. Place in oven until red beads attach to base; remove from oven and let cool. Hang from wide ribbon tied with a generous bow.

Ribbons of Red

This most dramatic and dazzling hue dresses up a home in festive fashion for Christmas.

Ribbons and Bows

The front door offers a glimpse of what awaits inside. Fresh greenery beribboned in red creates festive fanfare right from the start.

Check It Out

Vibrant red is a happy color that's most fitting for the season. From drapery to candlesticks, red accents bring a sense of joy. To dress up chairs for a special holiday gathering, tie sprigs of greenery to chair backs with pretty ribbon bows.

Home Sweet Home

Wondering how to keep gingerbread houses fresh? Store them in large glass containers, such as cookie and pickle jars. Settle the houses on sugar "snow" and surround the jars with miniature tree figurines. You don't make gingerbread houses? The look is just as cute using decorative paper houses. Make them glow in the snow by inserting battery-operated lights.

Tea Time

Be a prepared hostess by keeping a stash of spiced tea mix in a giant glass jar for guests to take home. Other surprises that will keep for weeks in small bags include wrapped candies or cookies, unpopped popcorn, hot chocolate packets, and, for pup owners—dog treats. For nonfood gifts, try travel-size lotions in holiday scents, votive candles in holders, ornaments, potpourri, or Christmas music CDs.

Hung with Care

Commandeer clothes hooks that normally corral coats and backpacks to display bright red Christmas stockings. Use temporary stick putty to hold up nameplates with chalk paper inserts, and write a name on each paper. Wrap small packages with initial tags, prop in stuffed animals, candy canes, and snippets of greenery as toppers for the batting-stuffed stockings.

Wrapped with Love

Wide red ribbons tied in luxurious bows elevate plain white-paper packages to extraordinary. To add a dash of contrast, tuck a sprig of greenery under the ribbon, then thread the ribbon through a tag adorned with jolly script.

Seasonal Color

In a guest bedroom, toss on red bedding and highlight the scene with a large fresh wreath suspended from a curtain rod. Evergreen adds seasonal scent while metal initials make guests feel right at home.

Night Light

Perk up a bedroom with a simple tree bedecked with red ribbons and lights. Authentic or simply props, packages in red and white add to the festive display.

Room in the Inn

When guests overflow from the main dining area, set up an equally inviting spot elsewhere. A long stretch of black chalkboard paper inscribed with "The First Noel" lyrics makes an extra-special table runner. Tie nametags to cloth napkins or take-home gifts using a generous amount of red ribbon. Mini rosemary trees nestled in burlap sacks spruce up the table for dinner and do double duty as party favors.

Recycling Style

Skip the recycle bin and reuse plastic bottles to make clever napkin rings, favors, and decorations.

Topsy Turvy

Dome cloches can be quite costly, but these little guys create the look for pennies. Cut off the bottom of a plastic beverage bottle. Invert and hot-glue a couple beads to the top. For the base, cut a circle slightly larger than the bottle opening using decorative-edge scissors. Glue a small church ornament, bottlebrush tree, or other tiny holiday trim in the center of the base. Center and glue the dome onto the base. Glue chenille stem around the edge.

Bottoms Up

Plastic beverage bottles often have designs impressed into them. Cut off the bottom of beverage bottles and smooth edge as for napkin rings, below. Fill with paper shred and candies for quick party favors.

Press and Polish

A semi-rigid water bottle is enough to make a set of napkin rings. Decide on a width, then use rubber bands to section increments as shown in Photo A. Cut the rings using scissors as shown in Photo B; remove rubber bands. Set a dry iron to high. To smooth the edges, one at a time carefully hold each plastic ring against the iron (wear an oven glove if desired), moving continuously in a circular motion until edges curl under, as shown in Photo C. For polka-dots, dab dots of white nail polish inside the ring; let dry. Brush red nail polish over entire inside of ring and let dry.

Minty Fresh

For subtle color, use a pretty pastel palette this season. Snowmen and playful pinecone friends remain festive well into the new year.

Friendly Atmosphere

Smiles all around! Playful characters, big and small, beckon guests to the table and start the conversation flowing. Choose a limited color scheme for a cohesive look; using various tones of one color palette is calming and refined. Gold or silver accents add glimmer.

Charming Charger

Plate chargers make place settings dramatically special. To further enhance the display, drill two holes approximately ½ inch from a charger edge. Thread with ribbon and tie into a bow. Hot-glue a large jingle bell in the center.

Trims

Pinecone Playmates

Make new friends to perch on the tree and play on the table. For each, hot-glue a wooden bead to the end of a pinecone. Use a fine-line permanent marking pen to draw a face using photos for inspiration. For arms and legs, use short pieces of chenille stems and glue into place. Add details using yarn for hair, felt for hats, scarves, bows, and shoes, beads for buttons, and floss for bows.

Simple Sensation

A brush of white paint and a sprinkle of glitter dress ordinary pinecones for a tree. Before painting, drill a tiny hole in the end of each pinecone then twist a mini screw eye into the hole. If necessary, secure with a dot of glue. Brush the pinecone with white paint, sprinkle on glitter, and let dry. Thread a wire hanger through the screw eye and tie on a ribbon bow.

Trims

Frosty Ornaments

Small round jars with lids take on a snowman shape from the get-go. Choose lightweight jars so tree branches can hold them without drooping. Drill a small hole in the lid and thread with ribbon for a hanger; knot ends on underside of lid. Twist lid tightly onto jar. Brush decoupage medium onto the jar and immediately sprinkle with white glitter; let dry. Use hot glue and buttons to attach nose, eyes, and smile. Tie a strip of felt around the lid to resemble hat trim.

Plate Pal

This friendly favor smiles at guests all evening long, then travels home with them. To make one, brush decoupage medium on a round jar with a lid. Immediately sprinkle with white glitter; let dry. Use hot glue to attach buttons and/or beads for nose, eyes, and smile. From mint green felt cut a circle approximately 2 inches larger than lid (doesn't have to be perfect to become a floppy-brimmed hat). Cut out a circle in the center, slightly smaller than the lid. Pull donut shape over lid. Hot-glue chenille stems around edges of brim. For adornment, hot-glue a red bead to one side of brim. Twist off the base of a small bottlebrush tree and hot-glue it in the bead opening. To highlight facial features, brush on a little white paint. Dip the handle in paint and make two dots on each eye. To prevent glitter from getting on the plate, set the favor in a paper baking dish.

Beverage Service

Carry out the pastel theme at the beverage bar with containers—even bottles—that blend in. Compatible color keeps the decorating scheme cohesive while introducing new flavors.

Old-Fashioned Flavor

Retro-packaged gums and candies add fun nostalgia and unusual color and graphics to Christmas tree branches. To hang, simply tie with coordinating ribbon and slip a wire hanger under the bow.

Trims

Simply Quaint

If you don't fill stockings, yet want the charm, call on these quick-to-make versions. Using the pattern on page 157, cut a pair of shapes from fabric using pinking shears. With wrong sides together, machine stitch ¼ inch from the edge. Hand-sew a ribbon hanger and bow to the top edge, heel side. For sturdier stockings that can be filled, adhere fusible web to back sides before cutting.

Ombre Trees

Subtly shaded trees are a pretty backdrop for seasonal trims. To achieve the ombre look, wear a plastic glove and hold a white bottlebrush tree by the base. In a well-ventilated work area, spray-paint the tree with mists of light green from bottom to about center; immediately sprinkle with glitter. Let the paint dry.

Clearly Christmas

Clear resin preserves charming seasonal symbols.

Merry Magnets

Following resin manufacturer's instructions, mix the catalyst with the resin as shown in Photo A, making enough to fill the tin shape. Slowly pour about ¼ inch of mixture into the mold as shown in Photo B. Place a sticker into the mold as shown in Photo C. Slowly pour more resin mixture into the mold to just below the rim, as shown in Photo D. Allow the mixture to harden per instructions. Hot-glue a magnet onto the back of the tin.

Tree Tins

Wonderfully nostalgic, these tins add a sense of yesteryear hanging from tree branches. To prepare a tin for hanging, drill a small hole approximately ¼ inch from the edge. Loop chenille stem and thread the ends into the hole; twist to secure. Seal the hole with a dot or two of hot glue on the outside of the tin. Add a sticker and resin as for magnets; let resin harden. Dip the open edge of the tin into decoupage medium then sprinkle with silver glitter; let dry. Brush away any excess glitter on face of ornament.

Trophy Winner

Carefully snip the blossoms (which are actually leaves called bracts) from a poinsettia plant—the stems are delicate and break easily. Paired with seeded eucalyptus and red pepper berries in a trophy-shape vase, these cream-and-pink dames make a winning design.

Arranged Elegance

Create showstopping floral displays by snipping and arranging these fresh holiday beauties.

Christmas Cranberries

Poinsettias with ruffled bracts lend a playful mood. A pair of red bracts cut from an inexpensive plant easily stand when held in place by fresh cranberries in glass jars. Here, stems are tucked into small vials of water that are hidden by the berries.

Trims

Holiday Heirloom

Arranged in an antique serving piece, cardinal-hue poinsettias pair with evergreen cuttings for traditional red-and-green display. To create arrangements as shown, stretch pieces of tape (any kind will do) across the top of a container in a grid then insert stems into openings. Tape holds each stem vertically in the vessel. Cut stems from a poinsettia are too delicate to insert into florist's foam.

Merry Magnolia
A glass cylinder lined with real or artificial southern magnolia leaves (showing brown undersides) holds a second container inside, where the cut ends of gorgeous cream-color poinsettia bracts stand.

Midas Touch New Year

Bring home the gold with playful and sophisticated accents that easily replace traditional Christmas hues and ornaments.

Playful Accents
Away with the holiday balls and ornaments. Replace December gems with kraft paper flowers in various sizes for New Year celebrations. To make the flowers, see instructions, opposite.

Gilded Accents

Shiny gold and matte kraft paper marry for a wonderful shabby chic look. To gold-leaf kraft paper, unroll a section on a flat surface. Randomly brush on imperfect swaths of crafts glue with a foam brush; do not coat entire surface with glue. Allow glue to set until tacky, then apply gold leaf sheets by gently rubbing in place with your finger. Remove gold leaf from unglued areas by gently dusting with a dry foam brush.

To make flowers, use the pattern on page 155 to cut shapes from gilded kraft paper. Fold each in half along the dotted lines as shown on the pattern. Unfold then fold in half along other axis; unfold. Glue a gold bead in the center of each flower.

To make holly ornaments, (below right) use pattern on page 155 to cut eight holly leaves from gilded kraft paper and fold each in half lengthwise with a bone folder. Glue one side of a folded leaf to one side of another. Repeat, stopping short of gluing first and last leaves together. Sandwich a loop of ribbon inside leaves and leave a 1-inch tail; glue first and last leaves. Tie a bead to each end of the ribbon.

Trims

Getting Glitzy

Simple stocking gift bags are a fun alternative to gift wrap. Cut a pair of stocking shapes from kraft paper (trace and enlarge a cookie cutter outline if pattern is needed). Add stripes or a grid with glue pen then apply gold leaf over the glue. Stitch or glue front and back pieces together.

Winning Combination

Carry out the gilded theme throughout the house with flowers (see page 85) attached to golden branches, party crackers, and crowns. The flowers attach securely using glue dots. Christmas crackers, a British tradition, make a pop and candy falls out when partners each pull one end of a cracker. The person holding the larger end gets the treats. These versions are made from a paper towel roll and kraft paper. To make crowns to wear when the clock strikes 12, cut a 3-inch strip from kraft paper, long enough to fit head. Cut points on one edge. Gild one side of the cutout. Tape the ends together on the inside to make a crown.

Terrific Take-Homes

Sending little gifts home with guests? Dress them up! Wrap gifts in paper decorated with metallic paint pens or gold leaf. Handmade paper tassels add a playful touch to a traditional gift box. To make a tassel, cut ½-inch-wide strips of plain kraft paper into twelve 10-inch lengths. Lay strips in a starburst pattern, gluing each strip to one on top. Let dry. Loosely bend bundle of strips in half to form a tassel. Glue a strip of gold-leafed kraft paper around bundle, 1 inch from bended top. For hanger, slip ribbon through the opening where strips are folded.

Table Matters

Holly & Ivy

Snuggle in to an intimate dinner with traditional holiday hallmarks in a red and green. Holiday china evokes childhood visions of Santa and his sleigh, while warm woolen mittens cradle utensils. Driftwood, tartan plaids, and pewter accents hint at New England winters by the fire. Cut pine peeks out of a lunch box for an inexpensive centerpiece. For variation, mix in cut flowers or berries.

Game Changer

Even adults will love the lighthearted look of this brunch table decor. Conversation is more likely to turn toward nostalgic Christmas mornings than social media posts when classic board games are used as place mats and a Christmas cracker (crafted from scrapbooking paper) is the 10-point place card. Taking cues from the color scheme of the board, settings are solid red, yellow, and white.

Wintry Wonder

White china—a cupboard staple—takes a casual tone with woodland accents. Lacy-edge plates stack up for a playful setting bookended by log slices—a charger and a nifty place card (both sizes readily available at crafts stores). Shaved-bark trees offer a miniature forest for a tabletop stag. Formal silver lends shimmer, while a jingle bell napkin ring calls for a toast.

Gold Standard

A gold charger resembling woven twigs nests this simple white dinner plate trimmed in gold. On top, a delightful goldfinch perches on a pretty package trimmed with forest pine and a hand-stamped Christmas greeting. The setting is backed with chevron wrapping paper as a table runner.

White Christmas

Add sparkle to an evening gathering with a mix of glittery silvers against a snowy white backdrop. A woven silver place mat lays the foundation for an art frame and a silver-and-white snowflake plate. Silver glitter snowflakes, reindeer, and jingle bells add to the wintry setting. Use a silver pen to write each guest's name on an office supply label, then use ribbon to tie each one to a ball ornament and bell for festive place-card favors.

Pistachio Bars
Recipe on page 115

food

THE HOLIDAY TABLE

Recipes for Success

Foods enjoyed just once a year make any occasion extra-special. From a casual soup and bread supper to an elegant appetizer buffet, you'll find just what you're looking for to entertain deliciously this season.

Snow-Capped Pie
Recipe on page 110

Appetizer Buffet

A tantalizing array of hot and cold finger foods provides a satisfying spread while encouraging guests to circulate and socialize all evening.

Chicken Sake Skewers

Chicken Sake Kabobs

A marinade of pineapple juice, sake, soy sauce, brown sugar, sesame oil, and crushed red pepper flavors these crunchy chicken kabobs.

PREP 20 minutes   MARINATE 1 hour
BAKE 12 minutes at 450°F
COOK 20 minutes

WHAT YOU NEED
1   cup unsweetened pineapple juice
¾   cup sake
¼   cup soy sauce
3   tablespoons packed brown sugar
3   tablespoons toasted sesame oil
½   teaspoon crushed red pepper
2   pounds skinless, boneless chicken breast halves, cut lengthwise into 1-inch-wide strips
1   cup peanut butter
½   cup half-and-half
1½ cups finely chopped cashews
     Asian sweet chili sauce

WHAT YOU DO
1. For marinade, in a small saucepan combine pineapple juice, sake, soy sauce, brown sugar, sesame oil, and crushed red pepper. Bring just to boiling over medium heat, stirring until brown sugar is dissolved. Reduce heat; simmer, uncovered, 20 minutes. Cool to room temperature.
2. Place chicken in a large shallow dish. Pour marinade over chicken; stir gently to coat. Cover and marinate in the refrigerator 1 to 2 hours, stirring once.
3. Soak 26 to 30 six-inch wooden skewers in water at least 30 minutes; drain before using. Preheat oven to 450°F. Lightly grease a 15×10×1-inch baking pan.
4. Drain chicken, discarding marinade. Pat chicken dry with paper towels. In a small bowl combine peanut butter and half-and-half. Place cashews in a shallow dish. Thread each chicken strip lengthwise onto a soaked skewer. Brush chicken with peanut butter mixture; roll in cashews to coat. Place in prepared baking pan. Bake about 12 minutes or until chicken is no longer pink, turning once.
5. Serve chicken kabobs with Asian chili sauce. Makes 26 servings.

Panko-Roasted Asparagus

Panko-Roasted Asparagus

Panko bread crumbs coat these extra-crispy green spears. If you like, use lemon-pepper bread crumbs for additional flavor.

PREP 20 minutes
ROAST 12 minutes at 425°F

WHAT YOU NEED
1   pound thick asparagus spears
½   cup mayonnaise
¼   cup Dijon mustard
2   teaspoons lemon juice
1   cup panko bread crumbs
2   tablespoons peanut oil

WHAT YOU DO
1. Preheat oven to 425°F. Snap off and discard woody bases from asparagus. If desired, scrape off scales. In a small bowl combine mayonnaise, mustard, and lemon juice. Transfer half the sauce to a small serving bowl; cover and chill until ready to serve.
2. Place bread crumbs in a shallow dish. Spread the remaining sauce on asparagus spears; roll in bread crumbs to coat. Place in an ungreased 15×10×1-inch baking pan. Drizzle with oil.
3. Roast about 12 minutes or until asparagus is crisp-tender and bread crumbs are golden brown. Serve asparagus with reserved sauce. Makes 16 servings.

Food

Roasted Pepper Queso Fundido

Roasted Pepper Queso Fundido

This cheesy, spicy, and indulgent dip will disappear quickly. Serve it with tortilla chips or crudités.

PREP 35 minutes
BAKE 20 minutes at 425°F
STAND 15 minutes

WHAT YOU NEED
2   fresh poblano chile peppers*
1   small red sweet pepper
3   cups shredded Monterey Jack cheese with jalapeño peppers (12 ounces)
2   tablespoons all-purpose flour
⅓   cup finely chopped onion
1   tablespoon butter
½   teaspoon ground cumin
¾   cup half-and-half
⅓   cup chopped peeled jicama
      Half-and-half (optional)
      Blue tortilla chips, scoop-shape tortilla chips, or corn chips

WHAT YOU DO
1. Preheat oven to 425°F. Quarter poblano peppers and sweet pepper lengthwise; remove stems, seeds, and membranes. Place pepper pieces, cut sides down, on a foil-lined baking sheet. Bake 20 to 25 minutes or until skins are blistered and dark. Bring foil up around peppers to enclose. Let stand 15 minutes or until cool. Using a sharp knife, loosen edges of skins; gently pull off skin in strips and discard. Finely chop peppers.
2. In a large bowl stir together cheese and flour; set aside. In a medium saucepan cook onion in hot butter over medium heat until tender. Add cumin; cook and stir 1 minute. Stir in the ¾ cup half-and-half.
3. Gradually add small amounts of cheese mixture, stirring constantly over low heat until cheese is melted. Stir in roasted peppers and jicama; heat through. If necessary, stir in additional half-and-half to make dip desired consistency. Serve dip with chips. Makes 12 servings.
*Test Kitchen Tip Chile peppers contain volatile oils that can irritate skin and eyes. Wear plastic or rubber gloves when working with them.

Parmesan-Stuffed Dates

The combination of sweet, smoky, and salty flavors in these stuffed dates makes them irresistible. Serve warm, not hot.

PREP 20 minutes
BAKE 12 minutes at 400°F

WHAT YOU NEED
12   fresh Medjool dates (about 12 ounces)
2   ounces Parmigiano-Reggiano cheese, cut into 12 small pieces
6   slices bacon, halved crosswise

WHAT YOU DO
1. Preheat oven to 400°F. Using a sharp knife, slit each date and remove the pit. Stuff each date with a piece of cheese. Wrap each with a bacon half and secure with a wooden toothpick. Place stuffed dates in a 15×10×1-inch baking pan.
2. Bake 12 to 14 minutes or until bacon is crisp. Serve warm. Makes 12 servings.

Bagna Cauda

The name of this recipe means "hot bath" in Italian and refers to the dipping sauce of butter, garlic, anchovies, and olive oil.

START TO FINISH 15 minutes

WHAT YOU NEED
⅓   cup olive oil
1   2-ounce can anchovy fillets, drained
2   cloves garlic, sliced
1   cup butter, cut up
      Assorted vegetable dippers (such as green beans, packaged peeled baby carrots, mushrooms, thinly sliced zucchini, broccoli florets, and/or cauliflower florets), blanched*

WHAT YOU DO
1. In a blender or food processor combine oil, anchovies, and garlic. Cover and blend or process just until anchovies and garlic are finely chopped.
2. Pour anchovy mixture into a small saucepan. Add butter. Cook over medium-low heat until bubbly, stirring occasionally.
3. If desired, keep warm in a 1½-quart slow cooker on low-heat setting up to 2 hours. Serve dip with vegetables. Makes 24 servings.
*Test Kitchen Tip To blanch vegetables, first cook them in boiling, lightly salted water 2 minutes; drain. Immediately plunge vegetables into a bowl of ice water; cool. Drain well.

Parmesan-Stuffed Dates

Veggie Spring Rolls with Chimichurri Sauce

Veggie Spring Rolls with Chimichurri Sauce

Fresh and light, these rice paper wraps combine an Asian concept with the savory flavors of chimichurri, a flavorful Argentinian herb sauce.

PREP 30 minutes   STAND 15 minutes

WHAT YOU NEED

1	recipe Chimichurri Sauce
1	cup shredded romaine lettuce
¾	cup packaged coarsely shredded carrots
½	cup bite-size strips zucchini
½	cup bite-size strips peeled jicama
2	green onions, cut into thin bite-size strips
6	8-inch rice papers
6	sprigs fresh Italian parsley

WHAT YOU DO

1. Prepare Chimichurri Sauce. In a medium bowl combine half the Chimichurri Sauce, the lettuce, carrots, zucchini, jicama, and green onions. Let stand 15 to 30 minutes to allow vegetables to soften slightly and absorb flavor from sauce, stirring occasionally. Cover and chill remaining sauce until ready to serve.

2. To assemble each roll, pour warm water into a pie plate. Carefully dip a rice paper into the water; remove to a clean kitchen towel. Let stand several seconds to soften. Place a parsley sprig in the center of the paper. Spoon about ⅓ cup of the vegetable mixture offset from center. Tightly roll rice paper from the lower edge, tucking in one side as you roll.

3. Serve spring rolls with remaining sauce. Makes 6 servings.

Chimichurri Sauce In a blender or food processor combine 1½ cups lightly packed fresh Italian parsley; ¼ cup olive oil; ¼ cup rice vinegar; 6 cloves garlic, minced; ¼ teaspoon salt; ¼ teaspoon black pepper; and ¼ teaspoon crushed red pepper. Cover and pulse until chopped, but not puréed.

Make-Ahead Directions Prepare as directed. Layer spring rolls between damp paper towels in an airtight container. Store in refrigerator up to 4 hours. Store remaining sauce in the refrigerator up to 4 hours.

Phyllo-Crusted Cheese with Bruschetta Topper

Phyllo-Crusted Cheese with Bruschetta Topper

Miniature cheese round wrapped in phyllo and baked until cheese is melted and pastry is crisp and flaky is finished with bruschetta topping.

PREP 30 minutes
BAKE 8 minutes at 400°F
COOL 10 minutes

WHAT YOU NEED

	Nonstick cooking spray
8	sheets frozen phyllo dough (14×9-inch rectangles), thawed
12	miniature wax-wrapped light semisoft cheeses, unwrapped
1	teaspoon dried Italian seasoning, crushed
¼	teaspoon black pepper
1	recipe Bruschetta Topping or ¾ cup refrigerated bruschetta topping plus 2 teaspoons white or regular balsamic vinegar

WHAT YOU DO

1. Preheat oven to 400°F. Lightly coat twelve 2½-inch muffin cups with cooking spray.

2. Unfold phyllo dough; place one sheet of phyllo on a clean work surface. (As you work, cover remaining phyllo dough with plastic wrap to prevent it from drying out.) Lightly coat phyllo with cooking spray. Top with another sheet of phyllo; coat with cooking spray. Repeat with two more sheets of phyllo, coating each with cooking spray. Cut phyllo stack in half lengthwise. Cut each half-stack crosswise into thirds (six rectangles total). Press each rectangle into a prepared muffin cup. Repeat to make six more phyllo cups, using remaining phyllo and coating each sheet with cooking spray.

3. Coat insides of phyllo cups with cooking spray. Place a cheese round in each phyllo cup. Sprinkle with Italian seasoning and pepper.

4. Bake about 8 minutes or until phyllo is golden brown. Cool in pan on a wire rack 10 minutes. Remove phyllo cups from muffin pan. Spoon Bruschetta Topping into phyllo cups. Serve warm. Makes 12 servings.

Bruschetta Topping In a medium bowl combine ½ cup chopped pitted kalamata olives; ¼ cup chopped tomato; 1 tablespoon snipped fresh basil; 1 tablespoon chopped bottled roasted red sweet pepper; 1 tablespoon chopped green onion; 1 tablespoon finely chopped carrot; 1 tablespoon finely chopped celery; 1 tablespoon olive oil; 1 teaspoon snipped fresh parsley; 1 teaspoon lemon zest; 1 teaspoon balsamic vinegar; 2 cloves garlic, minced; ⅛ teaspoon salt; ⅛ teaspoon dried oregano, crushed; and ⅛ teaspoon black pepper.

Soup & Bread Suppers

Holidays present the ideal time to put on fancy parties. Yet when you want something low-key, it's time to invite friends and family in for a spread of homey comfort foods.

Herbed Boule

Herbed Boule

Watch rising time carefully: The dough for this bread rises faster than many other yeast breads.

PREP 40 minutes
RISE 1 hour 5 minutes
STAND 10 minutes
BAKE 22 minutes at 450°F

WHAT YOU NEED
5½ to 6 cups all-purpose flour
2 packages active dry yeast
2 teaspoons salt
2 cups warm water (120°F to 130°F)
2 tablespoons snipped fresh thyme, snipped fresh sage, and/or snipped fresh rosemary
Cornmeal
1 egg white, lightly beaten
1 tablespoon water
2 cups ice cubes

WHAT YOU DO
1. In a large bowl stir together 2 cups of the flour, the yeast, and the salt. Add the 2 cups warm water to the flour mixture. Beat with an electric mixer on low to medium for 30 seconds, scraping side of bowl constantly. Beat on high for 3 minutes. Stir in thyme and as much of remaining flour as you can.
2. Turn dough out onto a lightly floured surface. Knead in enough remaining flour to make a stiff dough that is smooth and elastic (8 to 10 minutes total). Shape dough into a ball. Place in a lightly greased bowl, turning once to grease surface. Cover; let rise in a warm place until double in size (about 40 to 45 minutes).
3. Punch dough down. Turn dough out onto a lightly floured surface. Divide dough in half. Cover; let rest 10 minutes. Meanwhile, lightly grease a baking sheet; sprinkle with cornmeal.
4. Shape each dough portion into a 6-inch round loaf. Transfer dough rounds to prepared baking sheet. Cover; let rise in a warm place until nearly double in size (25 to 30 minutes).
5. Adjust one oven rack to lowest position and another oven rack to lower-middle position. Set a shallow baking pan on the bottom rack. Preheat oven to 450°F. Using a sharp knife, make an X in the top of each loaf. In a small bowl combine egg white and the 1 tablespoon water; brush tops of loaves. Place baking sheet with dough rounds on the lower-middle rack. Place ice cubes in the shallow baking pan (as they melt, they create steam and help dough rise and take on a crisp crust). Bake 22 to 25 minutes or until the loaves sound hollow when tapped. If necessary, cover baking pan with foil after 15 minutes to prevent overbrowning. Makes 24 servings.

Italian Wedding Soup with Escarole

Italian Wedding Soup with Escarole

This warming soup takes advantage of peak-season winter greens.

PREP 15 minutes
SLOW COOK 6 hours (low)

WHAT YOU NEED
2 eggs, lightly beaten
1 cup finely chopped onion (1 large)
⅓ cup fine dry bread crumbs
2 tablespoons grated Parmesan cheese
2 tablespoons snipped fresh Italian (flat-leaf) parsley
1 teaspoon salt
¾ teaspoon ground black pepper
1½ pounds lean ground beef
1 tablespoon vegetable oil
8 cups reduced-sodium chicken broth
3 large carrots, chopped
2 tablespoons snipped fresh oregano or 1½ teaspoons dried oregano, crushed
1 small head escarole (8 ounces), trimmed and cut into ½-inch strips
1 cup dried acini di pepe pasta
Fresh oregano sprigs (optional)

WHAT YOU DO
1. In a large bowl combine eggs, onion, bread crumbs, cheese, parsley, ½ teaspoon of the salt, and ½ teaspoon of the pepper. Add ground beef; mix well. Shape mixture into forty 1¼-inch meatballs. In a large skillet heat 1 tablespoon oil; brown meatballs, half at a time. Drain on paper towels.
2. In a 5- to 6-quart slow cooker, combine broth, carrots, dried oregano (if using), the remaining ½ teaspoon salt, and the remaining ¼ teaspoon pepper. Gently add meatballs.
3. Cover and cook on low-heat setting 6 hours or on high-heat setting 3 hours, stirring in fresh oregano (if using), escarole, and pasta during the last 20 minutes of cooking. Ladle into bowls. If desired, garnish with oregano sprigs. Soup will thicken upon standing. Makes 8 servings.

Homemade
Checkerboard Rolls

Homemade Checkerboard Rolls

Not only do these little breads have visual appeal, but everyone also gets to pick a favorite flavor—nutty seeds or crunchy cheese and cornmeal.

PREP **45 minutes**
RISE **1 hour 30 minutes**
STAND **10 minutes**
BAKE **12 minutes at 400°F**

WHAT YOU NEED
1   cup milk
¼   cup sugar
¼   cup butter
1   teaspoon salt
1   package active dry yeast
¼   cup warm water (105°F to 115°F)
1   egg, lightly beaten
3½ to 4 cups all-purpose flour
2   tablespoons sesame seeds
2   tablespoons poppy seeds
2   teaspoons dried minced onion and/or dried minced garlic
2   tablespoons yellow cornmeal
2   tablespoons grated Romano or Parmesan cheese
¼   cup butter, melted

WHAT YOU DO
1. In a small saucepan combine milk, sugar, ¼ cup butter, and the salt; stir over medium-low heat until warm (105°F to 115°F). Meanwhile, in a large bowl dissolve yeast in the warm water. Add the milk mixture and egg to yeast mixture. Gradually stir in enough flour to make a soft dough. Turn dough out onto a lightly floured surface. Knead in enough remaining flour to make a moderately soft dough that is smooth and elastic (about 3 minutes total). Shape dough into a ball. Place in a lightly greased bowl, turning once to grease surface. Cover and let rise in warm place until double in size (about 1 hour).
2. Grease a 15×10×1-inch baking pan; set aside. Punch dough down; turn out onto a lightly floured surface. Let dough rest 10 minutes. Divide dough evenly into 24 pieces. Gently shape into balls. In a shallow dish combine sesame seeds, poppy seeds, and dried minced onion. In another shallow dish combine cornmeal and Romano cheese. Place ¼ cup melted butter in a third dish. Working quickly, roll dough pieces in butter and in one of the seasoning mixtures to lightly coat. Coat half the rolls with one seasoning

mixture and half with the other. Alternate rolls in prepared pan. Cover rolls with greased plastic wrap and a towel. Let rise in a warm place 30 minutes.

3. Preheat oven to 400°F. Bake 12 to 15 minutes or until golden. Remove from pan. Serve warm or at room temperature. Makes 24 servings.

Test Kitchen Tip To keep the poppy seed topping out of the butter, coat all of the Romano cheese balls first. Place in alternating places on the pan. Next coat poppy seed rolls, filling in alternating spaces in the pan.

Whole Grain Caramelized Onion and Kale Bread

Infused with a wild combination of ingredients—whole wheat, oats, flaxseed, honey, pancetta, pear, kale, and garlic— this is truly a loaf fit for the holidays.

PREP **40 minutes**   RISE **1 hour**
CHILL **2 hours**   STAND **30 minutes**
BAKE **25 minutes at 350°F**

WHAT YOU NEED
3   ounces pancetta, chopped
1   tablespoon butter
1   cup chopped onion (1 large)
½   cup chopped ripe pear
6   cloves garlic, minced
2   cups chopped fresh kale
3½ to 4 cups all-purpose flour
1   package active dry yeast
1   teaspoon sea salt
1½ cups warm water (105°F to 115°F)
4   ounces Gruyère cheese, shredded
½   cup whole wheat flour
½   cup ground rolled oats*
½   cup flaxseed
1   egg
1   teaspoon honey
1   teaspoon water

WHAT YOU DO
1. In a large nonstick skillet cook pancetta over medium heat until crisp. Using a slotted spoon, transfer pancetta to a small bowl, reserving drippings in skillet. Add butter to drippings in skillet. Add onion, pear, and garlic; cook and stir about 5 minutes or until tender. Stir in kale and pancetta; cook until kale is tender. Remove from heat; cool.

2. In a large bowl combine 1 cup of the all-purpose flour, the yeast, and salt. Add

Whole Grain Caramelized Onion and Kale Bread

the 1½ cups warm water. Beat with an electric mixer on low to medium 30 seconds, scraping sides of bowl constantly. Beat on high for 3 minutes. Stir in cooled kale mixture and cheese. Using a wooden spoon, stir in whole wheat flour, ground oats, and flaxseed. Gradually stir in as much of the remaining all-purpose flour as you can.

3. Turn dough out onto a lightly floured surface. Knead in enough remaining all-purpose flour to make a moderately stiff dough that is smooth and elastic (6 to 8 minutes total). Shape dough into a ball. Place in a lightly greased bowl, turning once to grease surface. Cover; let rise in a warm place until double in size (about 1 hour).

4. Punch dough down. Turn dough out onto a lightly floured surface. Cover; let rest 10 minutes. Line a baking sheet with parchment paper; set aside. Shape dough by gently pulling it into a ball, tucking edges under. Place dough round on

prepared baking sheet. Flatten round slightly to about 9 inches in diameter. Cover. (To serve today, let rise in a warm place until nearly double in size [30 to 40 minutes]. Omit Step 5 and continue as directed in Step 6.)

5. Chill dough for at least 2 hours or up to 24 hours. Let stand at room temperature 30 minutes before baking.

6. Preheat oven to 350°F. In a small bowl whisk together egg, honey, and the 1 teaspoon water; brush top of dough round with egg mixture. Bake 25 to 30 minutes or until golden and bread sounds hollow when lightly tapped. Cool on a wire rack. Store in the refrigerator. Makes 16 servings.

***Tip** Place ⅔ cup rolled oats in a food processor or blender. Cover and process or blend to grind.

Classic Oyster Stew

Classic Oyster Stew

Many families—particularly in the Northeast—enjoy this rich seafood stew as a prelude to Christmas Eve church service. Taste it and see why the tradition has lasted for centuries.

START TO FINISH **25 minutes**

WHAT YOU NEED

3   ounces shucked oysters, undrained (about 1 pound)
4   cups whole milk
2   cups whipping cream
7   tablespoon unsalted butter
1   cup finely chopped yellow onion (1 large)
½   cup finely chopped celery (1 stalk)
¾   teaspoon kosher salt
3   tablespoons all-purpose flour
    Black peppercorns
    Dash cayenne pepper
    Snipped fresh parsley

WHAT YOU DO

1. Drain oysters, reserving liquor. Remove any shell pieces. Set aside oysters and liquor.

2. In medium saucepan heat milk and cream just to simmering; keep warm.
3. In Dutch oven heat 4 tablespoons of the butter over medium heat. When butter is melted and bubbling, add onion, celery, and ½ teaspoon of the salt, stirring well to coat in butter. Cook slowly, about 10 minutes, stirring often until onion is tender and translucent. Sprinkle flour over vegetable mixture. Cook 2 minutes more, stirring well to blend in the flour. Slowly whisk in the hot milk and cream; bring mixture back to a low simmer, stirring occasionally.
4. Meanwhile, in a 12-inch nonstick skillet heat remaining 3 tablespoons butter over medium heat until hot and bubbly. Add drained oysters in a single layer. Sprinkle with remaining salt and a few grinds of black pepper. Cook just until oysters begin to curl around the edges and gills are slightly exposed. Transfer oysters to the milk mixture in Dutch oven. Turn off heat.
5. Add oyster liquor to hot skillet. Cook 2 to 3 minutes, until boiling. Immediately transfer to stew in Dutch oven; stir. Stir in cayenne pepper. Cover and let stand 10 minutes. Sprinkle servings with parsley. Makes 10 servings.

Artisan Bread

Make this bread plain or try one of the stir-ins to make it sweet or savory.

PREP 25 minutes   CHILL 4 hours
STAND 30 minutes   RISE 1 hour
BAKE 25 minutes at 400°F

WHAT YOU NEED

¾   cup warm water (105°F to 115°F)
1   package active dry yeast
½   cup milk
2   tablespoons sugar
2   tablespoons butter or olive oil
1½   teaspoons salt
2¾   cups all-purpose flour
    Nonstick cooking spray or olive oil
    Cornmeal
1   egg
2   teaspoons water

WHAT YOU DO

1. In a large bowl stir together the ¾ cup water and the yeast. Let stand 5 minutes. Meanwhile, in a small saucepan heat and stir milk, sugar, butter, and salt just until warm (120°F to 130°F) and butter, if using, is almost melted. Stir milk mixture into yeast mixture until combined. Stir in flour (dough will be sticky). Lightly coat a medium bowl with cooking spray or brush with olive oil; transfer dough to the greased bowl. Lightly coat a sheet of plastic wrap with cooking spray or brush with olive oil; cover bowl with greased plastic wrap, coated side down. Chill at least 4 hours or up to 24 hours.
2. Using a dough scraper or spatula, carefully loosen dough from bowl and turn out onto a floured surface. Cover with greased plastic wrap. Let stand 30 minutes.
3. Grease a baking sheet; sprinkle lightly with cornmeal. Gently shape dough into a 6-inch round loaf, lightly flouring dough as needed. Transfer to prepared baking sheet, using dough scraper or spatula if necessary. Cover with a clean

kitchen towel and place on the middle rack of an unheated oven; place a bowl of warm water on the lower rack. Let rise until nearly double in size (about 1 hour).

4. Remove bread from oven; uncover and set aside. Preheat oven to 400°F. In a small bowl whisk together egg and the 2 teaspoons water; brush over loaf. Bake about 25 minutes or until an instant-read thermometer inserted in center of loaf registers at least 200°F. If necessary to prevent overbrowning, cover with foil the last 5 minutes of baking. Remove from baking sheet or pan; cool on a wire rack. Makes 12 servings.

Artisan Rolls Prepare as directed except shape dough into an 8-inch square. Cut into sixteen 2-inch squares, flouring dough and knife as necessary. Place about 1 inch apart on baking sheet. Bake about 15 minutes.

Stir-Ins In Step 1, add any of these ingredients with the milk mixture.

• ½ cup ground toasted almonds, ½ cup shredded smoked Gouda cheese (2 ounces), ¼ cup crisp-cooked and crumbled bacon, ¼ cup stone ground mustard, and 2 teaspoons toasted caraway seeds

• 1 cup chopped fresh or frozen rhubarb, ½ cup golden raisins, 2 tablespoons finely chopped shallot (1 medium), 2 teaspoons grated fresh ginger, and ½ teaspoon ground coriander

• ½ cup cooked mashed sweet potato and ½ teaspoon pumpkin spice. Reduce water in Step 1 to ½ cup.

• ½ cup crumbled feta cheese (2 ounces), ½ cup grated Asiago cheese (2 ounces), ¼ cup chopped pitted kalamata olives, ¼ cup thawed and well-drained chopped spinach, and 4 cloves garlic, minced

• ½ cup cooked chopped onion, ½ cup finely snipped dried apricots, ½ cup shredded Swiss cheese (2 ounces), and 1 teaspoon snipped fresh sage

Artisan Bread

Vegetable Cheese
Chowder

Vegetable Cheese Chowder

Even meat-eaters will enjoy this creamy, cheesy—and completely meat-free—soup.

START TO FINISH 25 minutes

WHAT YOU NEED

1   16-ounce package frozen broccoli, cauliflower, and carrots
½   cup water
2   cups milk
⅓   cup all-purpose flour
1   14.5-ounce can reduced-sodium chicken broth
1   cup shredded smoked cheddar or smoked Gouda cheese (4 ounces)
    Salt (optional)
    Ground black pepper
    Shredded cheese for topping

WHAT YOU DO

1. In a large saucepan combine frozen vegetables and the water. Bring to boiling; reduce heat. Simmer, covered, about 4 minutes or just until vegetables are tender. Do not drain.
2. Meanwhile, in a small bowl whisk together ⅔ cup of the milk and the flour until smooth. Stir flour mixture into vegetable mixture in saucepan. Add the remaining 1⅓ cups milk and broth. Cook and stir over medium heat until thickened and bubbly. Cook and stir 1 minute more. Remove from heat. Gradually add cheese, stirring until cheese is melted. Season to taste with salt (if desired) and pepper. Top servings with additional cheese, if desired. Makes 4 servings.

Steak and Potato Soup

A package of cooked beef roast au jus and a tub of chive-and-onion-flavor cream cheese make this elegant soup a snap to make.

PREP 20 minutes
ROAST 25 minutes at 425°F

WHAT YOU NEED

1   pound russet potatoes, peeled and cut into 1½-inch pieces
1   tablespoon olive oil
½   teaspoon ground black pepper
1   8-ounce tub cream cheese spread with chive and onion
3   cups 50% less sodium beef broth
1   17-ounce package refrigerated cooked beef roast au jus, broken into chunks
    Sour cream (optional)
    Snipped fresh chives (optional)

WHAT YOU DO

1. Preheat oven to 425°F. Place potatoes in a shallow roasting pan. Drizzle with oil and sprinkle with pepper; toss to coat. Roast, uncovered, 25 to 30 minutes or until potatoes are tender and browned on the edges, stirring occasionally.
2. Transfer potatoes to a large saucepan. Add cream cheese spread. Using a potato masher, coarsely mash potatoes, leaving some chunks. Add broth. Cook until cream cheese is melted, stirring occasionally.
3. Add beef chunks. Bring just to boiling; reduce heat. Simmer 5 to 10 minutes, gently stirring occasionally (try to avoid breaking up meat). If desired, top each serving with sour cream and sprinkle with chives. Makes 4 servings.

Caramelized
Shallot BLT Soup

Caramelized Shallot BLT Soup

The greens in this hearty BLT soup can be either chopped escarole or peppery arugula. You could also use more mild flavor spinach.

START TO FINISH **40 minutes**

WHAT YOU NEED

4   slices bacon
1½   cups sliced shallots (12 medium)
3   14.5-ounce cans reduced-sodium chicken broth
1   cup seeded and chopped roma tomatoes (3 medium)
2¼   cups coarsely chopped escarole or arugula

WHAT YOU DO

1. In a large skillet cook bacon over medium heat until crisp. Remove bacon and drain on paper towels, reserving 1 tablespoon drippings in skillet. Coarsely crumble bacon; set aside.
2. Add shallots to the reserved drippings. Cook, covered, over medium-low heat 13 to 15 minutes or until tender, stirring occasionally. Cook, uncovered, over medium-high heat 3 to 5 minutes or until golden, stirring frequently.
3. Transfer shallots to a large saucepan; add broth and tomatoes. Bring to boiling; reduce heat. Simmer 5 minutes. Stir in escarole; cook 5 minutes more. Top each serving with crumbled bacon. Makes 4 servings.

Popovers

The hot air of the oven works wonders on the simple mixture of eggs, flour, and milk. Crisp on the outside and custardy on the inside, these pillowy little breads are flavored with herbs, black pepper, and Parmesan cheese.

PREP **15 minutes**
BAKE **40 minutes at 400°F**

WHAT YOU NEED

1   tablespoon shortening or nonstick cooking spray
2   eggs, lightly beaten
1   cup milk
1   tablespoon olive oil
1   cup all-purpose flour
2   tablespoons grated Parmesan cheese

2   teaspoons finely snipped fresh
    sage or thyme or ½ teaspoon
    dried sage or thyme, crushed
½   teaspoon salt
½   teaspoon freshly ground black
    pepper

WHAT YOU DO

1. Preheat oven to 400°F. Using
½ teaspoon shortening for each cup,
grease the bottoms and sides of six
popover pan cups or 6-ounce custard
cups. (Or lightly coat with cooking
spray.) If using custard cups, place cups
in a 15×10×1-inch baking pan; set aside.
2. In a medium bowl combine eggs, milk,
and oil. Stir in flour until smooth. Stir in
cheese, sage, salt, and pepper.
3. Fill prepared cups half full with
batter. Bake about 40 minutes or until
very firm.
4. Immediately after removing from
oven, prick each popover with a fork to
let steam escape. Turn off oven. For
crisper popovers, return to oven for 5 to
10 minutes or until popovers reach
desired crispness. Remove popovers
from cups. Serve immediately. Makes
6 servings.

Spicy Tomato-Chicken Stew with Peanuts

*This African-style stew is a cinch to make
using a rotisserie chicken.*

START TO FINISH **30 minutes**

WHAT YOU NEED

2   tablespoons vegetable oil
½   cup chopped onion (1 medium)
1   tablespoon finely chopped fresh
    ginger
2   cloves garlic, minced
¾   cup creamy peanut butter
¼   cup tomato paste
2   teaspoons ground coriander
¼   teaspoon cayenne pepper
6   cups chicken broth
2   medium sweet potatoes (about
    1 pound), peeled and cut into
    1-inch pieces
1   14.5-ounce can diced tomatoes,
    undrained
3   cups shredded purchased
    roasted chicken
    Chopped peanuts (optional)
    Fresh cilantro leaves (optional)

WHAT YOU DO

1. In a large Dutch oven heat oil over
medium heat. Add onion, ginger, and
garlic; cook 5 to 6 minutes or until onion
is tender and beginning to brown,
stirring occasionally. Stir in peanut
butter, tomato paste, coriander, and
cayenne pepper. Cook and stir the
mixture 1 minute more.
2. Gradually stir in broth, sweet
potatoes, and tomatoes. Bring to boiling;
reduce heat. Simmer, covered, 20 to
25 minutes or until sweet potatoes are
tender. Stir in chicken; heat through. If
desired, garnish each serving with
peanuts and cilantro. Makes 6 servings.

Spicy Tomato-Chicken Stew with Peanuts

**Gingerbread
Snow Globe City**

Wintry Wonderland Sweets

Set a sparkly tone this season with these pretty and delicious treats created by pastry chef Gesine Bullock-Prado.

Salty-Sweet Snowflakes

In addition to the salt, the surprise ingredient in these buttery cookies is ground white pepper, which gives them a slightly spicy flavor.

PREP 45 minutes   CHILL 3 hours
BAKE 13 minutes at 350°F

WHAT YOU NEED
1	cup (2 sticks) unsalted butter, chilled
1	cup granulated sugar
1	egg
1	egg yolk
1½	teaspoons salt
1	teaspoon vanilla
1	teaspoon lemon zest
½	teaspoon ground white pepper
3	cups all-purpose flour
2	cups powdered sugar
1½	tablespoons meringue powder
2	to 3 tablespoons water

WHAT YOU DO
1. In a large bowl combine chilled butter and sugar. Beat butter and sugar with an electric mixture on medium-high until light and fluffy. Add egg and egg yolk; beat until fully incorporated. Add salt, vanilla, lemon zest, and white pepper. Slowly beat in flour. Using your hands, knead dough until smooth; divide in half. Wrap each dough half with plastic wrap; chill 3 hours.
2. Preheat oven to 350ºF. On a lightly floured surface, roll each dough half to ¼-inch thickness. Using a 4-inch snowflake cutter, cut out snowflakes. Arrange cutouts 1 inch apart on ungreased cookie sheets.
3. Bake 13 minutes or until edges just start to brown. Remove from oven. Cool on cookie sheets 5 minutes. Using a spatula, carefully remove cookies. Transfer to wire rack to cool completely. Decorate cooled cookies with Royal Icing. Makes 22 cookies.
4. While cookies cool, make Royal Icing. Stir together the powdered sugar, meringue powder and 2 tablespoons water in a small bowl. Stir, adding more water, 1 teaspoon at a time, until smooth. Spoon icing into a pastry bag fitted with a small round tip. Decorate cookies as desired. Let dry 15 to 20 minutes. Makes 22 cookies.

Gingerbread Snow Globe City

Capture a fantastical snow-covered village in a glass jar. The buildings are cut free-form with a paring knife.

PREP 1 hour   CHILL 30 minutes
BAKE 20 minutes at 350°F
STAND 30 minutes

WHAT YOU NEED
5	cups all-purpose flour
1	tablespoon ground ginger
1	teaspoon baking powder
1	teaspoon salt
1	teaspoon ground white pepper
1	teaspoon ground cinnamon
½	teaspoon ground nutmeg
1	cup (2 sticks) butter, softened
1	cup packed dark brown sugar
½	cup molasses
1	egg
½	cup milk
	Powdered sugar
	Granulated sugar

WHAT YOU DO
1. In a large bowl whisk together the flour, ginger, baking powder, salt, white pepper, cinnamon, and nutmeg until well combined; set aside.
2. In an extra-large bowl beat together the butter, brown sugar, and molasses with an electric mixer on high until light and fluffy. Add egg; beat until smooth and combined. Add half the flour mixture; beat just until combined. Add milk; beat just until combined. Add remaining flour mixture; beat just until combined. Using your hands, knead dough until smooth; divide in half. Wrap each dough half with plastic wrap; chill 30 minutes.
3. Preheat oven to 350°F. Roll each dough half on parchment paper to about a 15×10-inch rectangle. Using a sharp knife, score free-form building and rooftop shapes on each sheet of dough without cutting through dough. Using a cookie cutter, cut out trees. Transfer each parchment sheet of dough to a 15×10-inch baking pan. Remove excess dough scraps. Using the straight edge of a dough scraper or a knife, add brick, roof, and window scores without cutting through dough.
4. Bake 10 minutes. Remove from oven. Carefully cut along scored lines of building and roof shapes. Bake 10 minutes more or until firm. Remove from oven. Cool completely on a wire rack. Separate gingerbread pieces.
5. Sprinkle powdered sugar over cookies; gently rub in. Cover with waxed paper and let stand 30 minutes or up to 24 hours. Arrange cookies in a large glass jar filled with 2 to 3 inches of granulated sugar to stabilize cookies. Makes 72 servings.

Food

Snow-Capped Pie

A mountain of fruit gives this pie impressive height. (Pictured on page 91.)

PREP 40 minutes FREEZE 20 minutes
BAKE 1 hour 8 minutes at 350°F

WHAT YOU NEED

- ½ cup (1 stick) unsalted butter, softened
- ½ cup granulated sugar
- ½ teaspoon vanilla
- ½ teaspoon lemon zest
- 2 egg yolks
- 1½ cups all-purpose flour
- ½ teaspoon salt
  Nonstick cooking spray
- 4 tart apples (such as Granny Smith), peeled, cored, and sliced into ¼-inch wedges
- 3 ripe pears (such as Anjou), peeled, cored, and sliced into ¼-inch wedges
- 1 cup grated frozen purchased pound cake
- 1 cup dried cranberries
- ½ cup all-purpose flour
- ¼ cup packed brown sugar
- 2 teaspoons orange zest
- ½ 4-serving-size package instant vanilla pudding mix (3½ tablespoons)
- ½ cup whipping cream
- 2 tablespoons orange juice
- ½ 17.3-ounce package frozen puff pastry sheets (1 sheet), thawed
- 1 egg
- 1 tablespoon water
- 1 cup powdered sugar
- 4 teaspoon milk
  Maraschino cherry (optional)

WHAT YOU DO

1. For bottom crust, in a large bowl beat butter and sugar with an electric mixer on medium-high speed until light and fluffy. Add vanilla and lemon zest; beat just until combined, scraping down sides of bowl and necessary. Add egg yolks; beat until combined. Add flour and salt; beat just until dough just comes together. Using your hands, knead dough until flour is fully incorporated.

2. Coat a 9-inch fluted tart pan with removable bottom with nonstick cooking spray. Press dough into the bottom and sides of the pan. Cover with plastic wrap; freeze 20 minutes.

3. Preheat oven to 350°F. Bake crust, uncovered, 18 minutes or until edges just start to brown and bottom appears dry. Cool on wire rack.

4. In an extra-large bowl toss together apples, pears, cake crumbs, cranberries, flour, brown sugar, and orange zest; set aside. In a small bowl whisk together instant pudding mix, cream, and orange juice 1 minute or until well blended. Let stand 3 minutes until thickened. Stir pudding mixture into apple mixture. Mound filling into prepared crust*, leaving about ½ inch around the edge to tuck in pastry top.

5. Unfold puff pastry. On a lightly floured surface, roll out pastry to a 12-inch square. Carefully drape pastry over filling. Tuck edges of pastry between filling and bottom crust; trim excess pastry. In a small bowl combine 1 egg and 1 tablespoon water. Using a pastry brush, brush pastry with egg mixture. Transfer pan to a foil-lined baking sheet. Bake 50 minutes or until top crust is golden brown. Remove from oven. Cool completely on a wire rack.

6. For icing, whisk together powdered sugar and milk until smooth. Spoon half the icing over top of the pie; let stand 2 minutes. Spoon remaining icing over. Top with maraschino cherry, if desired. Makes 10 servings.

* If you place the filling in an 8-cup measuring cup, then invert it into the prepared crust, the mounding is done for you.

Pinecone Cakes

Layering the sliced almonds may be time-consuming, but the effect is magical.

PREP 1 hour
BAKE 18 minutes at 325°F

WHAT YOU NEED

- Nonstick cooking spray for baking
- 1⅔ cups all-purpose flour
- 1½ teaspoons baking powder
- ½ teaspoon salt
- ¼ teaspoon ground cinnamon
- ¼ cup whipping cream
- ½ cup (1 stick) unsalted butter, softened
- ½ cup granulated sugar
- ½ cup packed brown sugar
- 3 eggs
- 1½ teaspoons vanilla bean paste or vanilla
- ⅔ cup buttermilk or sour milk
- 1 8-ounce package cream cheese, softened
- ¼ cup (½ stick) unsalted butter, softened
- 2 cups powdered sugar
- ¼ teaspoon ground cinnamon
  Pinch salt
- 1 to 1½ cups sliced almonds, lightly toasted if desired
  Silver edible luster dust or powdered sugar (optional)
  Sweetened whipped cream (optional)

WHAT YOU DO

1. Preheat oven to 325°F. Coat each 4×3-inch cup of two 6-cup mini egg pans with nonstick spray for baking; set aside. In a medium bowl combine the flour, baking powder, salt, and cinnamon; whisk 30 seconds; set aside.

2. In a small bowl whisk the cream until stiff peaks form; set aside. In a large bowl beat the butter and sugars with an electric mixer on medium to high until light and fluffy, about 2 minutes, scraping bowl occasionally. Scrape down the bottom and sides of bowl. Add eggs, one at a time, mixing to just combine after each addition. Add vanilla bean paste and mix just until combined. Scrape the bottom and sides of bowl again and with the mixer on low, add half the flour mixture. Beat until combined. Add buttermilk, beating until combined (batter may appear curdled). Add remaining flour mixture, beating until combined. Fold in whipped cream.

3. Divide the batter among the egg cups, spooning ⅓ cup batter in each. Bake 18 to 20 minutes or until cake springs back when lightly touched. Cool in molds 5 minutes. Remove from oven. Cool completely on wire racks.

4. In a large mixing bowl beat cream cheese and butter until smooth. Add powdered sugar, cinnamon, and salt; beat on low until combined.

5. Frost each cake with about 2 tablespoons icing to coat, holding each from the bottom to ice. Arrange cakes on serving platters, then arrange almonds on frosted cakes in overlapping rows to resemble pine cones. If desired, use a small paintbrush to brush edges of nuts with luster dust, or sprinkle cakes lightly with powdered sugar. Serve with sweetened whipped cream, if desired. Makes 12 servings.

**Pinecone
Cakes**

Sweets to Share

Fill treat trays with homemade cookies, bars, and candies for neighbors and coworkers—or to enjoy at home.

Giant Nutmeg Cookies

As these soft and spicy cookies bake in the oven you'll enjoy the warm and welcoming fragrances of Christmas.

PREP 30 minutes
BAKE 13 minutes at 350°F

WHAT YOU NEED
1½ cups shortening
2 cups sugar
2 tablespoons grated whole nutmeg or 1 tablespoon ground nutmeg
2 teaspoons baking soda
1 teaspoon ground cinnamon
¼ teaspoon salt
2 eggs

Giant Nutmeg Cookies

½ cup molasses
4½ cups all-purpose flour
⅓ cup sugar
1 teaspoon grated whole nutmeg or ½ teaspoon ground nutmeg

WHAT YOU DO
1. Preheat oven to 350°F. In a large mixing bowl beat shortening with an electric mixer on medium to high for 30 seconds. Add the 2 cups sugar, the 2 tablespoons nutmeg, baking soda, cinnamon, and salt. Beat until combined, scraping sides of bowl occasionally. Beat in eggs and molasses until combined. Beat in as much of the flour as you can with the mixer. Using a wooden spoon, stir in any remaining flour.
2. In a small bowl stir together the ⅓ cup sugar and the 1 teaspoon nutmeg. Using a ¼-cup measure or cookie scoop, shape dough into 2-inch balls. Roll balls in sugar mixture to coat. Place balls 2½ inches apart on an ungreased cookie sheet.
3. Bake about 13 minutes or until tops are cracked and edges are firm (do not overbake). Cool on cookie sheet 2 minutes. Transfer cookies to a wire rack; cool. Makes 24 servings.

Chocolate-Caramel Clusters

These candy shop-quality treats could not be easier to make. It takes less than 30 minutes to assemble them, then they stand for 1 hour to set up. A sprinkle of coarse salt enhances their rich flavor.

PREP 20 minutes   STAND 1 hour

WHAT YOU NEED
1 8-ounce package pecan halves, toasted
1 14-ounce package vanilla caramels, unwrapped
1 tablespoon milk

1 12-ounce package dark chocolate pieces
2 ounces white baking chocolate with cocoa butter, chopped (optional)
1 teaspoon shortening (optional) Coarse sea salt or fleur de sel (optional)

WHAT YOU DO
1. Line a cookie sheet or tray with foil or parchment paper; grease foil or paper. For each cluster, on the prepared cookie sheet, arrange five pecan halves in a single layer close together.
2. In a small heavy saucepan stir caramels and milk over medium-low heat until mixture is smooth. Spoon caramel mixture over pecan clusters. Let stand about 30 minutes or until caramel is set.
3. In a medium-size heavy saucepan stir dark chocolate over low heat until melted and smooth. Remove ¼ cup of the melted chocolate; set aside. Spoon the remaining melted chocolate over clusters; gently spread chocolate to edges of clusters. Let stand about 30 minutes or until chocolate is set (if necessary, chill 5 to 10 minutes).
4. Meanwhile, if desired, in a small microwave-safe bowl combine white chocolate and shortening. Microwave on high about 1 minute or until melted and smooth, stirring every 30 seconds. Spread melted white chocolate in center of clusters.
5. Fill a small resealable plastic bag with reserved melted dark chocolate; snip a small hole in one corner of the bag. Drizzle dark chocolate over clusters. If desired, sprinkle with salt. Let stand until chocolate is set. Makes 20 servings.
To Store Layer clusters between sheets of waxed paper in an airtight container; cover. Store in the refrigerator up to 1 week.

Chocolate-Caramel Clusters

Peppermint Sandwich Crèmes

For festive flair, cream-cheese-peppermint filling is sandwiched between buttery shortbread coins.

PREP 30 minutes   FREEZE 2 hours
BAKE 10 minutes at 350°F

WHAT YOU NEED
½   cup butter, softened
1   cup sugar
¼   teaspoon baking soda
¼   teaspoon salt
1   egg
2   teaspoons vanilla
1   teaspoon peppermint extract
1¾ cups all-purpose flour
     Peppermint-Cream-Cheese
     Filling
     Finely crushed peppermint
     candies or sprinkles

WHAT YOU DO
1. In a large bowl beat butter with an electric mixer on medium to high 30 seconds. Add sugar, baking soda, and salt. Beat until combined, scraping bowl occasionally. Beat in egg, vanilla, and peppermint extract until combined. Beat in as much flour as you can with the mixer. Using a wooden spoon, stir in any remaining flour.
2. Divide dough into four portions. Shape each portion into an 8-inch roll. Wrap each roll in plastic wrap or waxed paper. Freeze 2 to 3 hours or until dough is firm enough to slice.
3. Preheat oven to 350°F. Unwrap dough rolls and cut into ⅜-inch slices. Place slices 1 inch apart on an ungreased cookie sheet. Bake 10 to 12 minutes or just until firm. Transfer cookies to a wire rack; cool.
4. Spread Peppermint-Cream-Cheese Filling on bottoms of half the cookies, spreading to edges. Top with remaining cookies, bottom sides together. Press lightly until filling comes just slightly over edges. Roll edges of cookies in crushed candies. Makes 35 servings.
Peppermint-Cream Cheese Filling
In a large bowl combine one 3-ounce package softened cream cheese and ¼ cup softened butter. Beat with an electric mixer on medium until smooth. Beat in 1 teaspoon vanilla and ½ teaspoon peppermint extract. Gradually beat in 3 cups powdered

**Peppermint
Sandwich Crèmes**

sugar. If necessary, beat in enough milk, 1 teaspoon at a time, to make filling spreading consistency. Makes 1⅔ cups.
To Store Layer filled cookies between sheets of waxed paper in an airtight container; cover. Store at room temperature up to 3 days or freeze up to 3 months.

Pistachio Bars

Two favorite flavors—pistachio and chocolate—come together in these chilled bars. (Pictured on page 90.)

PREP 35 minutes   CHILL 3 hours

WHAT YOU NEED
1   egg, lightly beaten
½   cup butter
¼   cup unsweetened cocoa powder
2   tablespoons granulated sugar
1   teaspoon vanilla
2   cups finely crushed cinnamon
     graham crackers
½   cup finely chopped pistachio
     nuts
¼   cup butter, softened
¼   cup pistachio instant pudding
     and pie filling mix
¼   cup half-and-half, light cream,
     or milk
1½   cups powdered sugar
6   ounces bittersweet chocolate,
     coarsely chopped
¼   cup butter
½   cup coarsely chopped pistachio
     nuts

WHAT YOU DO
1. Line a 9×9×2-inch baking pan with foil, extending foil over edges; set aside.
2. In a medium saucepan combine egg, the ½ cup butter, cocoa powder, granulated sugar, and vanilla. Stir over medium-low heat until butter is melted and mixture just starts to bubble. Remove from heat. Stir in crushed graham crackers and finely chopped pistachios. Press crumb mixture onto the bottom of prepared baking pan.
3. For filling, in a medium mixing bowl beat ¼ cup softened butter, dry pudding mix, and half-and-half with an electric mixer on medium until combined. Gradually add powdered sugar, beating well. Carefully spread filling over crust in pan. Cover and chill about 1 hour or until firm.

4. For topping, in a small saucepan stir chocolate and ¼ cup butter over low heat until melted. Spread topping over filling. Sprinkle with coarsely chopped pistachios. Cover and chill about 2 hours or until firm. Using edges of foil, lift uncut bars out of pan. Cut into bars. Makes 25 servings.
To Store: Layer bars between sheets of waxed paper in an airtight container; cover. Store in the refrigerator up to 3 days.

Almond-Sour-Cream Sugar Cookies

Sour cream gives these simple cookies extra-tender texture.

PREP 40 minutes   CHILL 1 hour
BAKE 7 minutes at 375°F

WHAT YOU NEED
⅔   cup butter, softened
1   cup sugar
1   teaspoon baking powder
½   teaspoon salt
¼   teaspoon baking soda
1   egg
⅓   cup sour cream
2   teaspoons vanilla
½   to 1 teaspoon almond extract
⅓   cup finely ground blanched
     almonds
2¼   cups all-purpose flour
     White or silver luster dust
     (optional)
1   recipe Royal Icing

WHAT YOU DO
1. In a large mixing bowl beat butter with an electric mixer on medium to high for 30 seconds. Add sugar, baking powder, salt, and baking soda. Beat until combined, scraping sides of bowl occasionally. Beat in egg, sour cream, vanilla, and almond extract until combined. Beat in ground almonds. Beat in as much flour as you can with the mixer. Using a wooden spoon, stir in any remaining flour. Divide dough in half. Cover and chill 1 to 2 hours or until dough is easy to handle.
2. Preheat oven to 375°F. On a well-floured surface, roll one dough portion at a time to ⅛-to ¼-inch thickness. Using 2½-inch cookie cutters, cut dough into desired shapes. Place cutouts 1 inch apart on an ungreased cookie sheet. Bake 7 to 8 minutes or until edges are

firm and bottoms are very light brown. Transfer cookies to a wire rack; cool.
3. If desired, use a small new paintbrush to brush cookies with luster dust. Pipe Royal Icing on cookies in snowflake designs. Let stand until icing is set. Makes 30 servings.
Royal Icing In a large mixing bowl stir together one 16-ounce package (4 cups) powdered sugar, 3 tablespoons meringue powder, and ½ teaspoon cream of tartar. Add ½ cup warm water and 1 teaspoon vanilla. Beat with an electric mixer on low until combined. Beat on high for 7 to 10 minutes or until icing is very stiff. If not using right away, cover bowl with a damp paper towel, then with plastic wrap. Chill up to 48 hours.
To Store Layer cookies between sheets of waxed paper in an airtight container; cover. Store at room temperature up to 3 days or freeze unfrosted cookies up to 3 months. To serve, thaw cookies, if frozen. Decorate as directed.

Slow-Cooker Warm-Ups

Eat, drink, and be merry! Count on your slow cooker to have festive beverages at the ready this season.

Bourbon-Citrus Sipper

In a 3½- to 4-quart slow cooker combine 6 cups apple cider or apple juice, ¼ cup sugar, 9 inches stick cinnamon, 8 whole cloves, and ½ teaspoon anise seeds. Cover and cook on low-heat setting 3½ to 4 hours or on high-heat setting 2 hours. Add 1 large naval orange, sliced, and 1 medium lemon, sliced. Cover and cook 30 minutes more. Place a fine-mesh sieve over a large bowl; strain cider. (Or use a slotted spoon to remove orange, lemon, and whole spices.) If using high-heat setting, turn cooker to low-heat setting. Return cider to slow cooker to keep warm. Just before serving, add ½ cup bourbon to cider. Makes 8 servings.

Winter Mulled Ale

Press 10 whole cloves into an orange in vertical rows. Cut orange into wedges with cloves in the center of each wedge. In a 3½- to 4-quart slow cooker combine orange wedges; three 12-ounce cans ale; one 12-ounce bottle ginger beer or ginger ale; and 8 inches stick cinnamon, broken. Cover and cook on low-heat setting 5 to 6 hours or on high-heat setting 2½ to 3 hours. Remove orange wedges and cinnamon, pressing wedges against sides of slow cooker to release juice. In a small bowl beat 3 egg yolks. Gradually whisk ½ cup of the hot ale into egg yolks. Return egg yolk mixture to cooker, whisking until frothy. Cook and whisk 1 minute more. Ladle into mugs. Add 1 or 2 sugar cubes to each serving. Makes 6 to 8 servings.

Bourbon-Citrus Sipper

Winter Mulled Ale

Silky Raspberry Hot Chocolate

Steaming
Pomegranate-
Ginger Tea

Mulled
Riesling
Punch

Silky Raspberry Hot Chocolate

In a 3½- or 4-quart slow cooker stir together 4 cups half-and-half or light cream and 4 cups whole milk. Cover and cook on low-heat setting for 5 to 6 hours or on high-heat setting for 2½ to 3 hours. If necessary, skim and discard "skin" from surface. Stir in one 12-ounce package bittersweet chocolate pieces and ½ cup milk chocolate pieces. Whisk until chocolate is melted and mixture is smooth. Serve immediately or keep warm, covered, on warm or low-heat setting up to 2 hours. Just before serving, stir in ½ cup raspberry liqueur or raspberry beverage flavoring syrup and 1 tablespoon vanilla. Makes 12 servings.

Steaming Pomegranate-Ginger Tea

In a 5- to 6-quart slow cooker combine 4 cups water; 2½ cups pomegranate beverage blend; 1½ cups dry red wine or additional pomegranate beverage blend; 1½ cups apple cider or apple juice; ½ cup sugar; two 2-inch pieces fresh ginger, peeled; and one 3-inch stick cinnamon. Cover and cook on low-heat setting for 5 to 5½ hours or on high-heat setting for 2½ to 3 hours. Turn off cooker. Add tea bags; let stand 2 minutes. Remove and discard tea bags. Makes 10 servings.

Mulled Riesling Punch

In a 3½- or 4-quart slow cooker combine one 750-mililiter bottle Riesling or other white wine, 2 cups apple cider or apple juice, and ¼ cup honey. In the center of a double-thick, 6-inch-square of 100-percent cotton cheesecloth, place a 1-inch piece of fresh ginger, thinly sliced, 12 whole allspice, and 8 whole cardamom pods. Bring up corners; tie closed with clean kitchen string. Add spice bag to cooker. Cover and cook on low-heat setting 3 to 4 hours or on high-heat setting 1½ to 2 hours. (Do not boil.) Stir in ½ cup Calvados or brandy. If desired, garnish drinks with cinnamon sticks and apple slices. Makes 6 to 8 servings.

gifts
FROM THE HEART

Make Them Memorable
Warm someone's heart with a custom gift
that shows how very much you care.

joy to the world

Let it

Hot Stuff

Make an impression—and functional works of art—using a wood-burning pen on a variety of surfaces.

Word Play

Remind yourself to slow down and live purposely with an inspirational message burned on a wood-slice plaque and then detailed with paint. Photocopy the "Live Simply" lettering and the black lines of the flower design on page 153. Place transfer paper on the wood-slice plaque then lay the pattern on top, ensuring lettering is straight. Trace the pattern using a ballpoint pen. Place the flower pattern near the top edge, allowing room for painting; trace black lines. Trace the letters using a wood-burning tool fitted with a flow point. Using the photo as a guide, burn branch lines using a cone point. Use a shading point to randomly burn leaves along the length of the branches by pressing the flat edge into the wood. Paint the flower branches and leaves as desired; let dry. For more detail, add more wood-burning on the flowers. Extend the technique to other accessories by adorning baskets with wood-burned labels that ensure holiday mail lands in its proper place.

Low Profile

Create a set of coordinating coasters by burning shapely silhouettes of people and animals onto the centers of square wooden plaques. Free downloadable silhouettes are available online or you can design your own. To make one, lightly trace a shape onto the center of a wooden plaque using a pencil. Trace the pencil lines using a wood-burning pen fitted with a narrow cone point. Use a flow point to fill in the outlines and burn the entire silhouette. Spray glossy polyurethane sealer on the coaster; let dry. Repeat with a second coat. Paint the beveled edges of the coaster; let dry.

Sweet Stuff

If your freehand lettering skills are shaky, use wood-burning letter tips to create professional-looking words. Mark the center of a canister lid with a pencil, then measure and mark letter placement on each side of the center point. Starting with the center letter, lightly press the wood-burning tool on top of the lid for 1 to 2 seconds. Let the tip cool at least 5 minutes before unscrewing it with needlenose pliers and replacing it with the next letter tip. Place tips on a heat-resistant surface to cool. For cooking utensils, use your imagination to customize wooden spoons, spatulas, and more. If you need a guide, lightly draw a design using a pencil then erase the marks when the wood-burning is complete.

The Write Stuff

Wood-burning pens needn't be limited to wood. Make your mark on a leather journal cover by burning a stamped image to create an embossed effect. First stamp the image with washable ink, then trace over the lines with the hot pen.

Strung Together

Experiment with a variety of wood-burner tips to freehand-draw dots, lines, squiggles, and letters onto colored wooden beads and a blank disc. String them together to make a pendant necklace. To make this disc design, transfer the pattern from page 152 onto the disc.

Tastes of the Season

For stuffing a stocking or presenting as a hostess gift, prettily wrapped homemade treats are always welcome.

Cranberry-Orange Caramel Corn, page 130

Christmas Cones

So merry and easy to tuck into a stocking, these cute cones take just minutes to make. Wrap a cardboard cone, available at crafts stores, with decorative paper, trim to fit, and adhere with a glue stick. Hot-glue tinsel garland around the opening. If desired, glue a row of buttons down one side. Tuck a triangular icing bag into the cone, fill with popcorn mix, and tie closed with ribbon.

Jingle Bell Tins

Tins not only make pretty presentations, they also keep candy fresh. To trim one, trace around the lid onto holiday paper; cut out. Glue the cutout to the lid using decoupage medium; let dry. Shape and hot-glue metallic chenille stem around the edge of the paper. Tie a ribbon bow; hot-glue to top of paper with a jingle bell in the center of the bow.

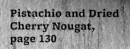

**Pistachio and Dried
Cherry Nougat,
page 130**

Snowman Cake Pops

These cute little guys (and gals!) have personality-plus! Let your creativity loose when decorating these whimsical cake pops. Baking and decorating them is a terrific family activity.

PREP **1 hour**
FREEZE **1 hour to 1 hour 30 minutes**
STAND **at least 30 minutes**

WHAT YOU NEED

1 package 2-layer-size white cake mix
1 to 1½ cups Basic Butter Frosting*
12 ounces vanilla-flavor candy coating, chopped
12 ounces white baking chocolate, chopped
16 lollipop sticks
1 cup chopped flaked coconut or ⅓ cup coarse white sugar
32 pretzel sticks
Assorted candies for decorating**

WHAT YOU DO

1. Prepare cake mix according to package directions, using any suggested pan size. Cool completely in pan on a wire rack. Line trays or baking sheets with waxed paper.

2. Remove cooled cake from pan and crumble into an extra-large mixing bowl. Add desired amount of frosting. Beat with an electric mixer on low until combined. Using a small scoop, drop mixture into forty-eight 1-inch mounds onto prepared trays; roll mounds into balls and freeze 30 minutes.

3. In a small microwave-safe dish heat 1 ounce of the coating (about ¼ cup) on medium for 60 seconds until melted and smooth, stirring once. To assemble, dip one end of each lollipop stick into melted candy coating and poke stick into one ball, about 1½ inches of stick exposed at top. Add a second ball. Redip end of stick into melted coating; add the third ball. Freeze 30 to 60 minutes more or until balls are firm.

4. Place remaining candy coating and chopped white chocolate in a small saucepan. Heat over medium-low heat until melted and smooth, stirring frequently. Use a spoon to cover balls with melted coating-chocolate mixture, allowing excess to drip off. While wet, sprinkle with chopped flaked coconut. Insert pretzel sticks for arms. Insert lollipop sticks into florist's foam to stand pops upright; let stand until firm. Decorate as desired using assorted candies and a small amount of melted coating to attach candies to cake pops. After coating and decorations are set, transfer to storage containers and store, covered, in refrigerator. Let stand at room temperature at least 30 minutes before serving. Makes 16 pops.

Basic Butter Frosting In a medium mixing bowl beat ¼ cup softened butter with an electric mixer on medium until smooth. Gradually add ⅔ cup powdered sugar, beating well. Slowly beat in 2 tablespoons milk and ½ teaspoon vanilla. Gradually beat in 2 cups additional powdered sugar. If necessary, beat in additional milk, 1 teaspoon at a time, to make frosting of spreading consistency.

***Tip** If the higher amount of frosting is used, the cake balls will be rich and creamy but softer set. Make sure the balls are frozen solid, and work quickly when dipping.

****Tip** For a hat, roll out one large black gumdrop to ¼-inch thickness. Attach to another gumdrop using extra melted coating mixture.

Under Wraps

Clear plastic treat bags let the personalities of these cute characters shine through. Randomly place a few snowflake stickers on the bag, slip in the cake pop, and tie with a dainty ribbon bow. If desired, slip the packaged treat into a small stocking.

Pumpkin-Spiced Gingersnap Truffles, page 129

House Boxes

Give small boxes festive facelifts with holiday papers cut into house shapes. First cover the box lid with paper; use a glue stick to secure. Trim with roof, window, door, and chimney pieces. For trim, use white paper and decorative-edge scissors. Glue pieces in place. Add dimensional sticker details. Line the box with tissue paper before filling with truffles.

Can-Do Attitude

Recycle bin to the rescue! A clean can (with no sharp edges) makes a wonderful treat holder. Wrap it with print cardstock using hot-glue to secure. Hot-glue trim to the rim and add a ribbon bow and button. Place hot chocolate mix into a clear cellophane bag, seal with a twist tie, and place in the can.

Clever Crackers

These little surprise packages are just the right size to hold mini shortbread bites. Use tissue paper rolls or trimmed paper towel or wrapping paper tubes for cylinders. Place a clear cellophane treat bag into the tube and fill it with cookies; close with a twist tie. Wrap the tube with gift wrap, allowing 3 extra inches on both ends; tape seam in the center. Pinch the paper at tube ends; tie with ribbon. Add a holiday sticker to the center of the cracker.

Elfin Shortbread Bites, page 129

Pumpkin-Spiced Gingersnap Truffles

For a bit of variety, roll half the truffles in cocoa powder and half in crushed gingersnaps. To crush gingersnaps, place them in a plastic bag then roll and press with a rolling pin.

MICROWAVE 70 seconds
CHILL 2 hours 30 minutes
PREP 20 minutes

WHAT YOU NEED

1¼ cups semisweet chocolate pieces
¼ teaspoon pumpkin pie spice
¼ teaspoon vanilla
½ cup cream
¾ cup chopped gingersnaps (about 10 cookies)
⅓ cup finely crushed gingersnaps (about 7 cookies) and/or ¼ cup unsweetened cocoa powder

WHAT YOU DO

1. In medium bowl combine chocolate pieces, pumpkin pie spice, and vanilla.
2. In medium microwave-safe bowl place whipping cream. Microwave on high for 70 seconds or until boiling (or place cream in saucepan and bring just to boiling.) Pour cream over chocolate mixture. Let stand 5 minutes. Whisk until smooth. Stir in chopped gingersnaps. Cover; refrigerate 1½ to 2 hours or until firm but soft enough to form into balls.
3. Place crushed gingersnaps and/or cocoa powder in small bowl(s). Using a small spoon, shape 1-tablespoon portions of truffle mixture into balls. Roll in crushed gingersnaps or cocoa powder to coat. Refrigerate 1 hour or until firm. Store, covered, in refrigerator, up to 3 days. Makes 20 to 25 truffles.

Elfin Shortbread Bites

These tiny treats, studded with brightly colored candy sprinkles, are fun, festive and delicious. At just ½-inch square, they're perfectly sized to eat more than one!

PREP 20 minutes
BAKE 12 minutes at 325°F

WHAT YOU NEED

1¼ cups all-purpose flour
3 tablespoons sugar
½ cup butter
2 tablespoons colored sprinkles

WHAT YOU DO

1. Preheat oven to 325°F. In a medium bowl stir together flour and sugar. Using a pastry blender, cut in butter until mixture resembles fine crumbs and starts to cling. Stir in colored sprinkles. Form dough into a ball and knead until smooth.
2. On an ungreased cookie sheet roll or pat dough into an 8×5-inch rectangle. Cut into ½-inch squares. Separate squares on the cookie sheet.
3. Bake 12 to 14 minutes or just until the bottoms start to brown. Transfer to a wire rack covered with waxed paper and let cool.
4. Fill crackers as directed at left, "Clever Crackers." Makes 144 pieces (thirty-six 4-piece servings).
Make-Ahead Directions Place cookie bites in an airtight container; cover. Store at room temperature up to 3 days or freeze up to 3 months.

Decadent Hot Chocolate Mix

Each bag of this peppermint-flavor hot chocolate mix makes four servings. It's just right for stirring together after an afternoon of sledding or ice skating.

PREP 15 minutes
COOK 5 minutes

WHAT YOU NEED

1 cup sugar
1 cup unsweetened cocoa powder
2 cups nonfat dry milk powder
1½ cups semisweet chocolate pieces
1 cup crushed soft peppermint sticks

Decadent Hot Chocolate Mix

WHAT YOU DO

1. In three 1-pint plastic bags layer ingredients equally in the following order: sugar, cocoa powder, milk powder, semisweet chocolate pieces, and crushed peppermint sticks.* Seal bags and attach directions for making Decadent Hot Chocolate (see Step 2). Place bags in clean, recycled soup cans. See "Can-Do Attitude," left.
2. In a large saucepan combine bag contents with 1⅔ cups water. Heat and stir over medium heat until hot and chocolate pieces have melted. Pour into four mugs. If desired, serve with marshmallows. Makes 3 bags mix (4 servings each).
* Use a funnel or waxed paper or parchment paper rolled into a funnel when layering ingredients into the bags.
Make-Ahead Directions Store bags of mix in a cool, dry place up to 1 month.

Gifts

Cranberry-Orange Caramel Corn

Tuck a bag of this sweet and crunchy caramel corn into a stocking and you are sure to get a Christmas-morning kiss.

PREP 25 minutes
BAKE 30 minutes at 275°F

WHAT YOU NEED
12	cups popped popcorn
1	cup dried cranberries
½	cup whole almonds
½	cup butter
½	cup packed brown sugar
¼	cup light-color corn syrup
2	tablespoons orange juice
2	teaspoons vanilla
½	teaspoon baking soda

WHAT YOU DO
1. Preheat oven to 275°F. In an extra-large bowl combine popped popcorn, dried cranberries, and almonds; set mixture aside.
2. In a 2-quart saucepan stir the butter, brown sugar, and corn syrup over medium heat until butter is melted. Stir in the orange juice. Bring to boiling over medium heat. Boil at a moderate, steady rate 2 minutes. Remove from heat. Stir in vanilla and baking soda (mixture will foam up).
3. Pour the syrup mixture over the popcorn mixture; stir to coat well. Transfer to a 15×10×1-inch baking pan or a shallow roasting pan. Bake 30 minutes, stirring twice. Transfer caramel corn to a large heavy sheet of greased foil; let cool. Store caramel corn in covered containers. Makes 10 servings.

Pistachio and Dried Cherry Nougat

Each heavenly bite of this airy, chewy candy is studded with crunchy pistachios and tart dried cherries. (Shown page 125.)

PREP 1 hour
COOK 25 minutes   STAND 1 hour

WHAT YOU NEED
	Cornstarch
1½	cups sugar
1	tablespoon cornstarch
1	cup light-color corn syrup
½	cup water
2	egg whites
1	teaspoon vanilla
1½	teaspoons lemon zest
¾	cup chopped pistachio nuts
¾	cup dried tart red cherries

WHAT YOU DO
1. Line a 9×5×3-inch baking pan with foil, extending foil beyond edges of pan. Butter foil; sprinkle with a small amount of cornstarch. Set pan aside.
2. In a medium-size heavy saucepan combine sugar and 1 tablespoon cornstarch. Stir in corn syrup and water. Bring to boiling over medium-high heat, stirring constantly with a wooden spoon to dissolve sugar (5 to 7 minutes). Avoid splashing syrup on sides of pan. Carefully clip a candy thermometer to side of pan. Reduce heat to medium; continue boiling at a moderate, steady rate until thermometer registers 286°F, soft-crack stage (20 to 25 minutes). Adjust heat as necessary to maintain a steady boil.
3. Remove saucepan from heat. Remove thermometer. In a large bowl beat egg whites with an electric mixer on medium until stiff peaks form (tips stand straight). Gradually pour hot syrup in a very thin stream into egg whites, beating on high and scraping sides of bowl occasionally. Add syrup slowly to ensure proper blending (about 3 minutes).
4. Add vanilla. Continue beating on high until candy becomes very thick and less glossy, scraping sides of bowl occasionally (5 to 6 minutes). When beaters are lifted, candy should fall in a ribbon, mound on itself, then slowly disappear into remaining candy.
5. Immediately stir in lemon zest, pistachio nuts, and dried cherries. Quickly spoon candy into prepared pan. While nougat is warm, score into 2×¾-inch pieces. When firm, use foil to lift it from pan. Place on cutting board; cut into pieces. Wrap each piece in plastic wrap. Makes 48 servings.
To Store Place wrapped pieces in an airtight container; cover. Store at room temperature up to 2 weeks.

Beef 'n' Potato Dog Biscuits

Show your best buddy that you care by making homemade treats from Santa.

PREP 45 minutes
BAKE 1 hour at 300°F
COOL 30 minutes

WHAT YOU NEED
1	cup lower-sodium beef broth, warmed (105° to 115°F)
1	package active dry yeast
2¼	cups all-purpose flour
1½	cups whole wheat flour
1	cup cornmeal
½	cup toasted wheat germ
½	cup nonfat dry milk powder
1	teaspoon dried Italian seasoning
½	cup finely shredded potato
½	cup finely shredded sweet potato

WHAT YOU DO
1. Preheat oven to 300°F. Line a cookie sheet with parchment paper; set aside.
2. In a small bowl stir together broth and yeast; let stand 5 minutes. Meanwhile, in a large bowl stir together all-purpose flour, whole wheat flour, cornmeal, wheat germ, nonfat dry milk, and Italian seasoning. Using a wooden spoon, stir in yeast mixture, potato, and sweet potato. Turn dough out onto a lightly floured surface. Knead until gathered and smooth (dough will be very stiff).
3. On a well-floured surface roll dough to ¼-inch thickness. Using a 4-inch bone-shape cutter, cut dough into shapes. Place shapes on prepared cookie sheet.
4. Bake about 60 minutes or until golden on both sides. Turn off oven; cool in oven 30 minutes. Transfer biscuits to a wire rack. Makes about 30 biscuits.
To Store Place biscuits in an airtight container; cover. Refrigerate up to 1 month.

Jolly Jars

No one will mind dog treats on the counter when they're kept in such a darling jar! Use scrapbook trims for initials, letters, dog tags, or stickers to personalize a hand-cut paper tag. Use double-sided tape to adhere the tag and trims to the jar front. Add a ribbon around the jar top and finish with a generous bow.

G
gus
sweet
boy

Beef 'n' Potato Dog Biscuits

Gifts

Creative Coils

Transform cotton cording into pretty and practical accessories using a fun and easy coiling technique.

Room to Grow

Set a terra-cotta planter in a coiled cachepot that coordinates with the decor of a gift recipient.

WHAT YOU NEED

⅛ yard of green print fabric
Approximately 50 feet of
³⁄₁₆-inch cotton cord
Clear sewing thread
Clear-drying crafts glue

WHAT TO DO

1. Cut green print fabric into 1-inch strips.
2. Referring to how-to photos A, B, and C and using white sewing thread, sew between the cord rounds to make a 4-inch-diameter coil for the cachepot base.
3. To begin sides, lay the cord on top of the outermost base coil. Shift base under the sewing machine foot so the coil is flipped up vertically on the left side of foot. Continue sewing between cording until cachepot sides are 3 inches tall.
4. Wrap a green print strip clockwise around the cord, and continue sewing the coil two rounds, adding more green strips as necessary.
5. Continue sewing uncovered cord for the coil for approximately five more rounds or until sides are 4½ inches tall. Trim cord end, leaving 3 inches unsewn. Cover cut end with clear-drying crafts glue to prevent fraying; let dry. Sew remainder of cord to top of cachepot, backstitching at the end for reinforcement.

A. For a round base, coil one end of the cord tightly around itself a few times until the coil is the size of a quarter.

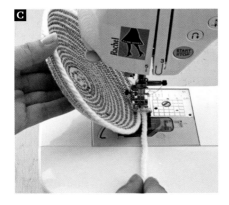

C. Slowly rotate coils counter clockwise as you zigzag-stitch between rows. For long continuous curves, you may wish to switch to an open tow sewing machine foot. Tilt the coil as you stitch to build the sides.

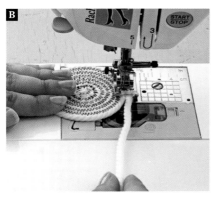

B. White holding coil firmly, place the coil under sewing machine zigzag foot, with cord extending to the right side. Use a wide zigzag to stitch between cording rows, catching cording on both sides to hold it together.

Cover a portion of the plain cording with decor-coordinating fabric to add rows of accent color.

Gifts

Tote-ally Awesome

What a functional yet decorative way for family and friends to stash stuff! Whip up a handled bag by stitching together sweater-wrapped clothesline. Create a long oval base, then shift the base under the sewing machine foot so the oval is flipped up slightly on the left side of the foot; continue adding rows to build the sides. This project uses approximately 100 feet of ¼-inch clothesline cord to make a bag that is 8 inches tall (with handles) by 17 inches wide.

Round About

Do the twist! Wrap clothesline cord with colorful 1- to 1½-inch strips cut from old sweaters, then zigzag-stitch it into a flat coil to make festive trivets. Leave a gap on opposite sides of the last two coil rounds to form handles. This project uses approximately 50 feet of ³⁄₁₆-inch cord. The handle is added after the coil reaches about 11 inches in diameter.

Hip to Be Square

These beauties are meant to protect tabletops. Shape fabric-covered ¼-inch clothesline cord in a back-and-forth pattern for the 4-inch-square core of each coaster, then use contrasting fabric to stitch border rows.

Beautifully Beribboned

Tiny Trees

Transform bits of ribbon into sensational tabletop trees. For the base, use a branch slice approximately 1½ inches tall and 1½ inches in diameter. Drill a hole in the center, large enough to fit a stick. Knobby sticks work well because the ribbons stay in place without slipping. Hot-glue the stick into the hole. Knot various green ribbons to the stick, trimming the ends at an angle, shorter toward the top of the tree. Tie a red ribbon bow at the top.

Merry Candle Mat

Give lighting a little lift with a ring of ribbon framing a candle cup. Use a metal ring, available in crafts and fabric stores, slightly smaller than the candleholder. Cut ribbon approximately 4 to 6 inches in length. To attach to ring, fold each ribbon in half. Slip the loop under the ring, then pull the ends through the loop. Pull snug to secure. Trim ends if needed.

Greeting Card Clips

Make a lively garland of holiday cards. To make the holders, carefully remove the clips from several clothespins. Use a glue stick to adhere ¼-inch ribbon to one side of clothespin, pressing into the clip groove; replace clip. Thread string through the holes, using a dot of hot glue to hold in place if needed.

Cheerful Rings

These whimsical napkin rings bring pure fun to the holiday table. Using an elastic ponytail band for the ring, tie snippets of ribbon around the band to cover. Use varying colors and widths for a whimsical look.

Ribbon-Wrapped Place Cards

A few snippets of ribbon transform plain place cards into fancy table trims. Fold 3×5-inch cardstock in half. Use a glue stick to secure ribbon pieces to the card fronts as shown, wrapping ends to the back. Write a name on the blank space of card.

LET 'EM GET CRAFTY
kids

Grow Some Smiles

Arm kids with simple crafts supplies and they'll be happy for hours making wonderful holiday decorations and unforgettable memories.

Jolly Trims

Paper pals, accented with dimensional trims, will spark kids' imaginations and keep their little hands busy, busy, busy.

All Smiles

This snow gal delivers merry messages. Trace the patterns on page 157; cut out. Use the patterns to cut card pieces. Cut a 10×8-inch white cardstock; fold in half short ends together. Adhere shapes in place, starting with background, then snow, snow gal, and clothing accents. Finish with buttons, tiny jingle bells, artificial holly leaves, and pom-poms.

Strut Your Stuff

This darling penguin adds a playful touch to the Christmas tree. Make a colony of these cute little guys and use your imagination to dress them up. To make one, trace the patterns on page 156; cut out. Use the patterns to cut pieces from cardstock. Adhere layers together with glue stick. Use thick crafts glue to attach the trims.

Let's Dance

Frolicking gingerbread guys and gals offer a cheery welcome. Trace the gingerbread cookie pattern on page 154; cut out. Trace around the pattern on brown cardstock; cut out. Outline each gingerbread character using a white marking pen; let dry. Trace clothing patterns on page 154, or cut your own. Use patterns to cut pieces from solid or patterned cardstock. Use a glue stick to adhere clothing. Use crafts glue to attach trims, such as pom-poms, buttons, ribbon, and more to embellish clothing and make faces. Draw a smile with black marking pen. Tuck the figures into a wreath and fill in with candy canes, small ornaments, and a ribbon bow.

Macaroni Magic

Available in a sleighful of shapes, pasta provides shape and texture for making wreaths, trees, snowmen, and snowballs.

Sparkling Snowballs

Full of texture and sparkle, these fancy snowballs won't ever melt. To make one, coat a plastic or satin ornament ball with thick white crafts glue or decoupage medium. Sprinkle with couscous to cover the surface. Add more glue and couscous if needed; let dry. Paint the snowball white then immediately sprinkle with white glitter; let dry. Hang the creations on a tree or nestle them in an arrangement of colorful ornaments.

Happy Snowman

With so many pasta shapes available, snowman expressions are limitless! Using a cardboard or wood circle as the base, glue couscous to one side, adding facial details with shapes of pasta. Paint all the pasta black and let dry. Paint the couscous white, allowing some black to show through. Paint the nose orange and the remaining details black. When dry, brush on white highlights and let dry.

All-Aglow Evergreen

Ruffle-edge lasagna noodles and a variety of pasta pieces add details to tiny trees.

WHAT YOU NEED

Tracing paper
Pencil
Scissors
Cardboard
Lasagna noodles
Hot-glue gun and glue sticks (or thick
    white crafts glue for young children
Shell, elbow, and star macaroni
Acrylic paint: black, green, metallic
    gold, yellow red, blue, purple, pink,
    white
Paintbrushes
Chenille stem

WHAT YOU DO

1. Trace the pattern on page 156 onto
tracing paper; cut out. Use pattern to cut
out the shape from cardboard.
2. Break lasagna noodles into different
lengths of wedge shapes to cover
cardboard shape. Break two small strips
to make the tree trunk. First glue the
two trunk pieces to the cardboard.
(Note: Older children can use a hot-glue
gun; younger children should use thick
white crafts glue.)
3. Start at the bottom of the tree with a
lasagna noodle long enough to cover
cardboard and glue it in place covering
the top of the tree trunk and lower edge
of the cardboard.
4. Add tree pieces, using shorter pieces
working toward the top of the tree.
5. Glue various macaroni shapes to the
tree as ornaments. Use star macaroni at
the top. Let the glue dry.
6. Paint the entire tree black using light
paint strokes; let dry. Paint the tree with
brushstrokes of medium and light green,
allowing black to remain in crevices. Let
the paint dry.
7. Paint the "ornaments" with different
colors. Make the elbow macaroni look
like candycanes by painting them white
with red stripes. Let all the paint dry.
8. Using very little white paint, brush
the tree edges to look like snow.
9. To add "lights," dip the paintbrush
handle in paint and dot on the tree. Use
several colors to make it lively; let dry.
10. Glue a ring made of chenille stem to
the back for hanging.

Merry Wreath

Full of texture, this clever mini wreath is made from spaghetti, shell macaroni, and bowtie pasta.

WHAT YOU NEED

Spaghetti

Hot-glue gun and glue sticks (or thick white crafts glue for children too young to use a glue gun)

6-inch flat wreath form

Shell macaroni, small and large

Bow tie pasta

Acrylic paint: black, dark green, light green, red, pink, metallic gold, white

Paintbrushes

Note: To hang the wreath on a wall, simply hook the wreath form over a nail. To use as a package trim or ornament, ask an adult to help predrill a hole near the top of the wreath form and insert a piece of ribbon before creating the wreath.

WHAT YOU DO

1. Break spaghetti into pieces approximately 1 inch long. As shown in Photo A, randomly glue pieces of spaghetti onto wreath form to cover.

2. Glue small shell macaroni "berries" on wreath as shown in Photo B.

3. Add a bow at the top made from a large piece of bow tie pasta topped with a large piece of shell macaroni. Paint the entire wreath black using light paint strokes as shown in Photo C; let dry.

4. Using a little green paint on the paintbrush, paint the tops of the spaghetti pieces as shown in Photo D; let dry. The black paint in the crevices will add dimension. Using very little light green paint, brush the tips of the spaghetti as shown in Photo E.

5. Coat the shell macaroni "berries" with red paint as shown in Photo F; let dry. Add a light brush stroke of pink on each berry as shown in Photo G. Paint the bow gold; let dry.

6. Use white paint to brush on snowy details as shown in Photo H; let dry.

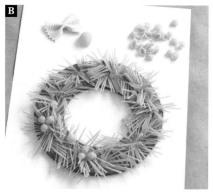

Sleek Wreath

Wooden beads offer a graphic twist on a traditional wreath. Hot-glue varying sizes of wooden beads ranging from ⅝ to 1½ inches in diameter) to the front of a flat wooden wreath ring. Glue on additional beads starting on the inside edge of the ring and finishing at the outer edge. Fill in gaps with smaller beads. Glue red felt balls on the front, and loop a ribbon around the wreath to hang.

Going with the Grain

Craft holiday magic by making projects using wooden balls and wood veneer paper.

Trees Two Ways

As ornaments or gift trims, little trees add handmade flair. Take your pick of shapes—a mod triangular tree with dot "ornaments" or a whimsical tree with scallops. (All patterns are on page 158.) For the triangular tree, trace the tree base pattern onto the wood veneer paper; cut out. Punch holes in the tree shape, using hole punches, where circles appear on the pattern. Glue the tree shape to felt; trim felt edges. Punch a hole in the top of the tree and loop thread through for hanging.

For a scallop tree, trace the patterns. Trace the tree base pattern onto wood veneer paper; cut out. Trace the scallop-edge top layer patterns onto wood veneer paper and felt (two wood veneer and three felt pieces per ornament) as noted on patterns; cut out. Glue the scallop-edge pieces to the tree base, starting at bottom and in order shown on patterns. Punch a hole in the top of the tree and loop thread through for hanging.

Winter Greetings

Modern takes on snowmen and greeting cards earn rave reviews for fresh style.

WHAT YOU NEED FOR THE SNOWMEN

Hot-glue gun and glue sticks
Wooden balls: 2, 2½, and 3 inches in diameter
Small hole punches
Felt scraps: red, tangerine, black
Wooden accessories for hats or stands, such as napkin
    rings, mini flowerpots, round disks, or eggcups
Pom-poms in desired colors
Fast-drying crafts glue, such as Beacon 3-in-1 adhesive

WHAT YOU DO

1. For each snowman, hot-glue two different-size wooden balls together to create a body.
2. Punch eyes and buttons from felt. For a nose, twist a tiny strip of orange felt, secure with glue, and trim into a triangular shape. Glue felt pieces to the body. Tie on a felt scarf.
3. Hot-glue the wooden accessories together to create a hat. Hot-glue hat to head. Adorn the hat with a felt band and/or pom-poms. If desired, prop a snowman on a stand.

WHAT YOU NEED FOR THE STITCHED CARDS

Light- or medium-weight wood veneer paper, such as
    BARC paper
Blank cards
Tree, snowflakes, or wreath pattern, page 158
Long heavy needle
Embroidery floss
Cardstock in colors of your choice
Fast-drying crafts glue, such as Beacon 3-in-1 adhesive
Scrap of ribbon for wreath

WHAT YOU DO

1. Cut a piece of wood veneer paper smaller than the front of a blank card. Place a pattern on the cut wood veneer paper atop a piece of heavy cardboard
2. Use the needle to poke holes through the pattern and wood veneer paper. Remove cardboard and pattern.
3. Stitch the design using a needle threaded with floss, asking an adult for help if needed. Tape floss ends to back of wood veneer paper.
4. Glue the stitched wood veneer paper to a piece of cardstock cut slightly larger than the paper. Glue to the card.
5. Embellish the wreath with a ribbon "bow" as shown above.

Colorful Snowflakes

Dreaming of a white Christmas? Instead, try a color-happy flurry of snowflakes. To make one snowflake, tape the corners of a sheet of lightweight veneer paper (such as BARC paper) to a work surface. Paint one side of the paper with acrylic paint thinned with water; let dry. Remove the tape. Cut the painted paper into ½×12-inch strips (or 8- and 10-inch strips for smaller snowflakes). Bend each strip to form a loop, painted side inside, glue ends together, and clamp with a clothespin; let dry. Remove clothespin. Glue 14 to 16 strips together, forming a circle; let dry. Glue circles punched from scraps of wood veneer paper to the center. Tie thread through a loop to hang.

Merry-Go-Round

Cool Coasters

Break out a hypotrochoid art set and watch kids' imaginations flourish! Gel pens offer several color choices and work well for these projects. Choose those that blend with your holiday decor. To make coasters, simply create round designs on white cardstock. Trace a circle around the motif and trim with decorative scissors.

Groovy Gift Wrap

Plain white kraft paper lets colorful hypotrochoid designs pop. Use a handful of pen colors and try out different wheel combinations to get a beautiful assortment of designs. Use the graphic paper as wrap for the most special holiday gifts.

Merry Place Cards

Let kids add their creative touch to the holiday table. To make place cards, draw decorative circles on white cardstock. Write names inside the circles and wrap the fold with metallic chenille stems.

Festive Place Mats

A few sheets of 11×17-inch paper to draw on and you'll have holiday place mats in no time. Let the kids be their own designers, making matching sets or individual works of art.

Fun Tree Trims

Trimmed with narrow borders, these circular designs make sweet ornaments. Write a meaningful word inside the circle before gluing on a metallic chenille stem "frame" and hanger.

Patterns

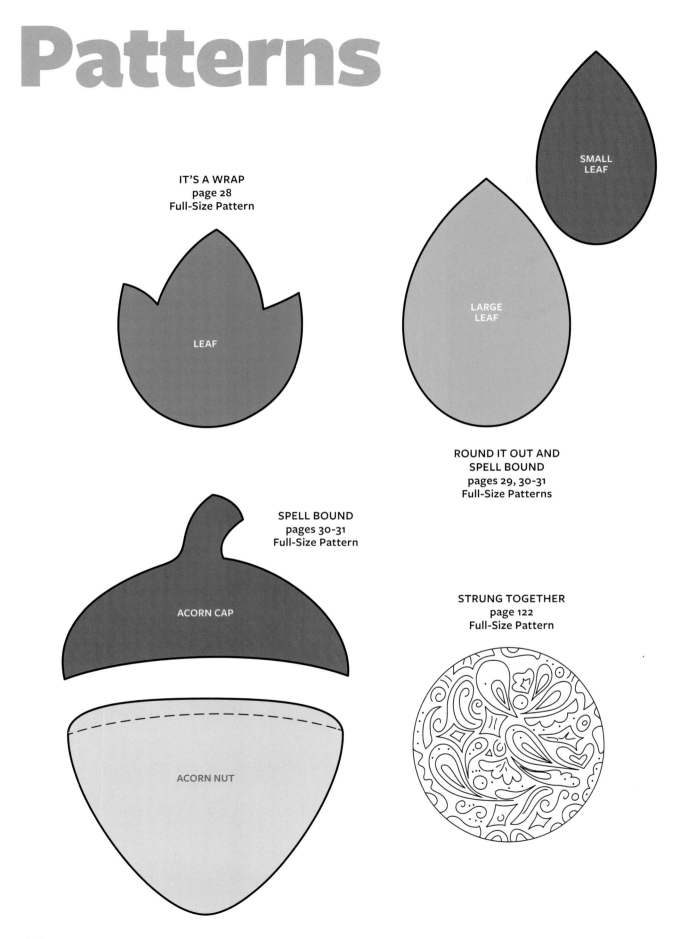

IT'S A WRAP
page 28
Full-Size Pattern

LEAF

SMALL
LEAF

LARGE
LEAF

ROUND IT OUT AND
SPELL BOUND
pages 29, 30-31
Full-Size Patterns

SPELL BOUND
pages 30-31
Full-Size Pattern

ACORN CAP

ACORN NUT

STRUNG TOGETHER
page 122
Full-Size Pattern

WORD PLAY
pages 120-121
Full-Size Pattern

Live Simply

WORD PLAY
pages 120-121
Full-Size Pattern

Patterns

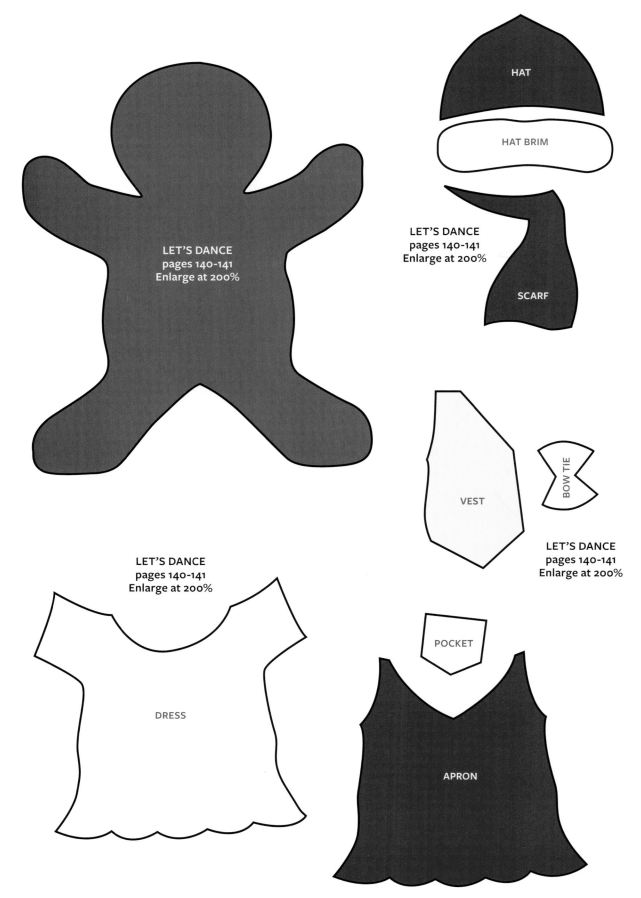

HAT

HAT BRIM

LET'S DANCE
pages 140-141
Enlarge at 200%

SCARF

LET'S DANCE
pages 140-141
Enlarge at 200%

VEST

BOW TIE

LET'S DANCE
pages 140-141
Enlarge at 200%

POCKET

LET'S DANCE
pages 140-141
Enlarge at 200%

DRESS

APRON

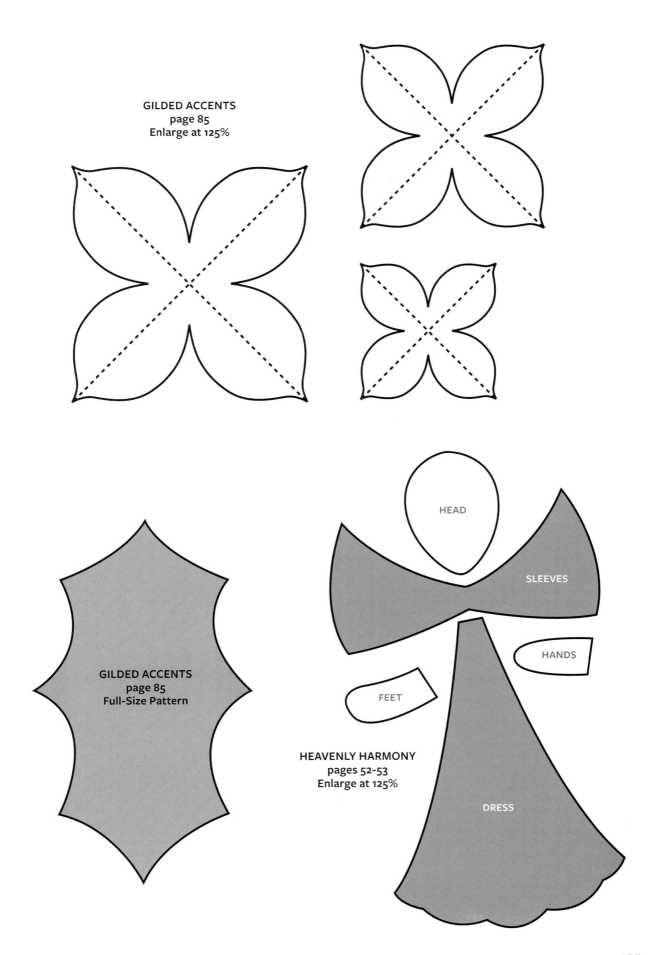

GILDED ACCENTS
page 85
Enlarge at 125%

GILDED ACCENTS
page 85
Full-Size Pattern

HEAD

SLEEVES

HANDS

FEET

HEAVENLY HARMONY
pages 52-53
Enlarge at 125%

DRESS

Patterns

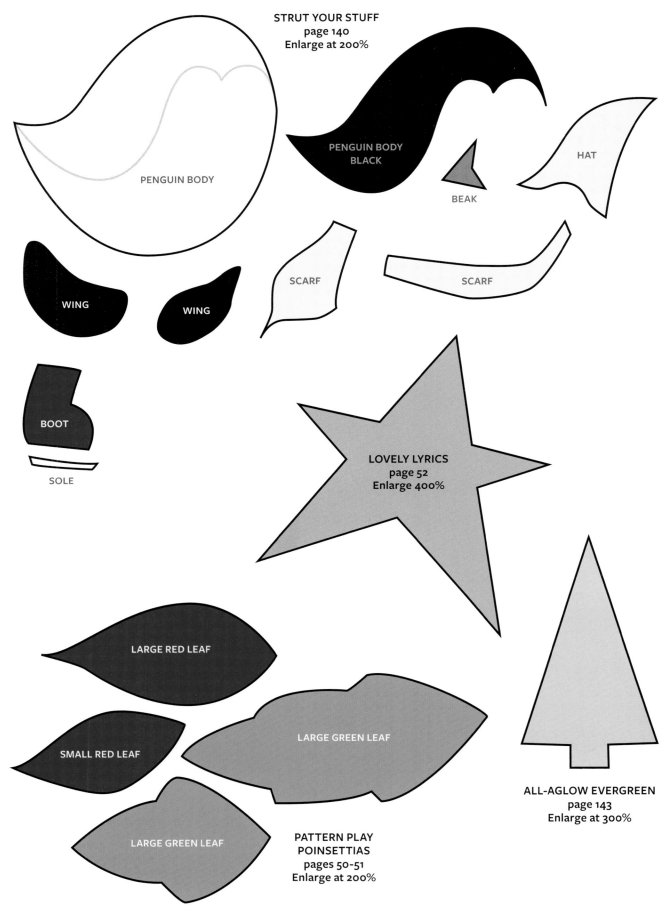

STRUT YOUR STUFF
page 140
Enlarge at 200%

PENGUIN BODY

PENGUIN BODY BLACK

BEAK

HAT

WING

WING

SCARF

SCARF

BOOT

SOLE

LOVELY LYRICS
page 52
Enlarge 400%

LARGE RED LEAF

SMALL RED LEAF

LARGE GREEN LEAF

LARGE GREEN LEAF

ALL-AGLOW EVERGREEN
page 143
Enlarge at 300%

PATTERN PLAY
POINSETTIAS
pages 50-51
Enlarge at 200%

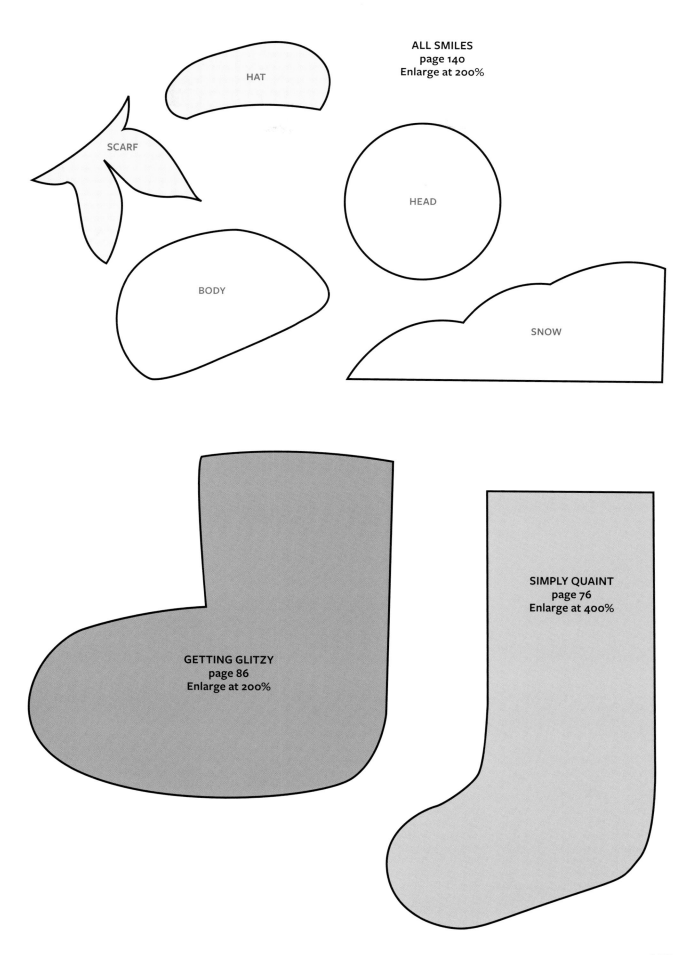

ALL SMILES
page 140
Enlarge at 200%

HAT

SCARF

HEAD

BODY

SNOW

GETTING GLITZY
page 86
Enlarge at 200%

SIMPLY QUAINT
page 76
Enlarge at 400%

Patterns

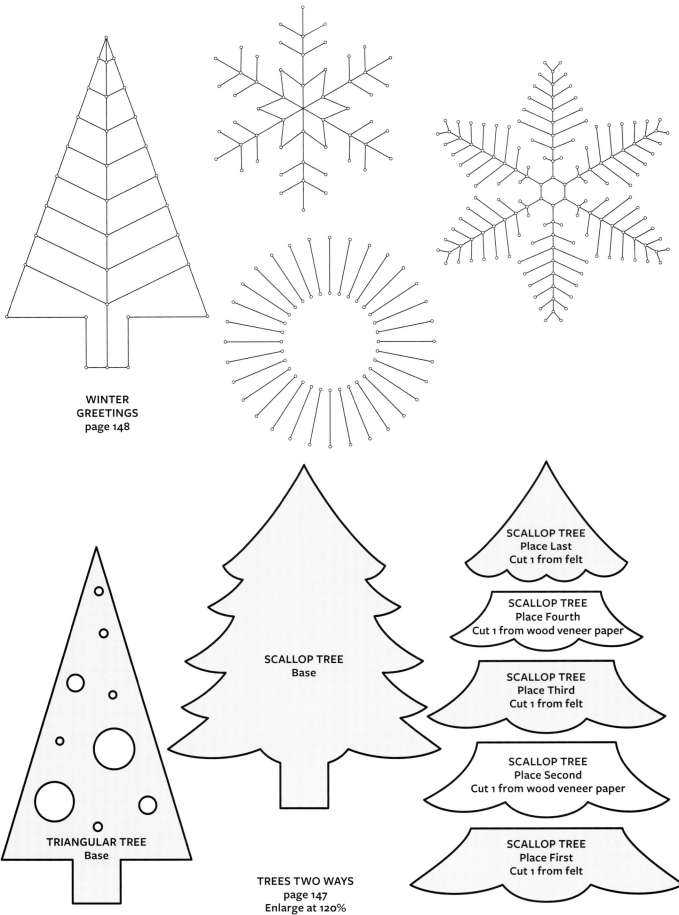

**WINTER
GREETINGS**
page 148

SCALLOP TREE
Base

SCALLOP TREE
Place Last
Cut 1 from felt

SCALLOP TREE
Place Fourth
Cut 1 from wood veneer paper

SCALLOP TREE
Place Third
Cut 1 from felt

SCALLOP TREE
Place Second
Cut 1 from wood veneer paper

TRIANGULAR TREE
Base

TREES TWO WAYS
page 147
Enlarge at 120%

SCALLOP TREE
Place First
Cut 1 from felt

Index

Index

CREDITS

Photo Styling
Sue Banker
Doug Samuelson

Photography
Jason Donnelly
Jacob Fox
Marty Baldwin